P9-DGN-500

DUE

GRAPHIC BIOGRAPHIES

CESAR CHAVEZ

FIGHTING FOR FARMWORKERS

by Eric Braun

illustrated by Harry Roland,
Al Milgrom, Steve Erwin,
and Charles Barnett III

Consultant:
Clete Daniel
Professor of American Labor History
School of Industrial and Labor Relations
Cornell University, Ithaca, New York

Capstone
press
Mankato, Minnesota

Graphic Library is published by Capstone Press,
151 Good Counsel Drive, P.O. Box 669, Mankato, Minnesota 56002.
www.capstonepress.com

Printed in the United States of America

1 2 3 4 5 6 10 09 08 07 06 05

Library of Congress Cataloging-in-Publication Data
Braun, Eric, 1971–
Cesar Chavez : fighting for farmworkers / by Eric Braun; illustrated by Harry Roland, Al Milgrom, Steve Erwin, and Charles Barnett III.
p. cm.—(Graphic library. Graphic biographies)
Includes bibliographical references and index.
ISBN 0-7368-4631-X (hardcover)
1. Chavez, Cesar, 1927—Juvenile literature. 2. Labor leaders—United States—Biography—Juvenile literature. 3. Migrant agricultural laborers—Labor unions—United States—Officials and employees—Biography—Juvenile literature. 4. Mexican American migrant agricultural laborers—Biography—Juvenile literature. 5. United Farm Workers—History—Juvenile literature. I. Title. II. Series.
HD6509.C48B72 2006
331.88'13'092—dc22 2005006460

Summary: Describes in graphic novel format the life of labor leader Cesar Chavez and the boycotts he led to gain fair working conditions for farmworkers.

Art and Editorial Direction
Jason Knudson and Blake A. Hoena

Designers
Jason Knudson and Jennifer Bergstrom

Colorist
Benjamin Hunzeker

Editor
Erika L. Shores

Editor's note: Direct quotations from primary sources are indicated by a yellow background.

Pages 15, 22, 25, from *The Fight in the Fields: Cesar Chavez and the Farmworkers Movement* by Susan Ferris and Ricardo Sandoval (New York: Harcourt Brace, 1997).
Page 17, from *Cesar Chavez: Autobiography of La Causa* by Jacques E. Levy (New York: W. W. Norton Company, 1975).

TABLE OF CONTENTS

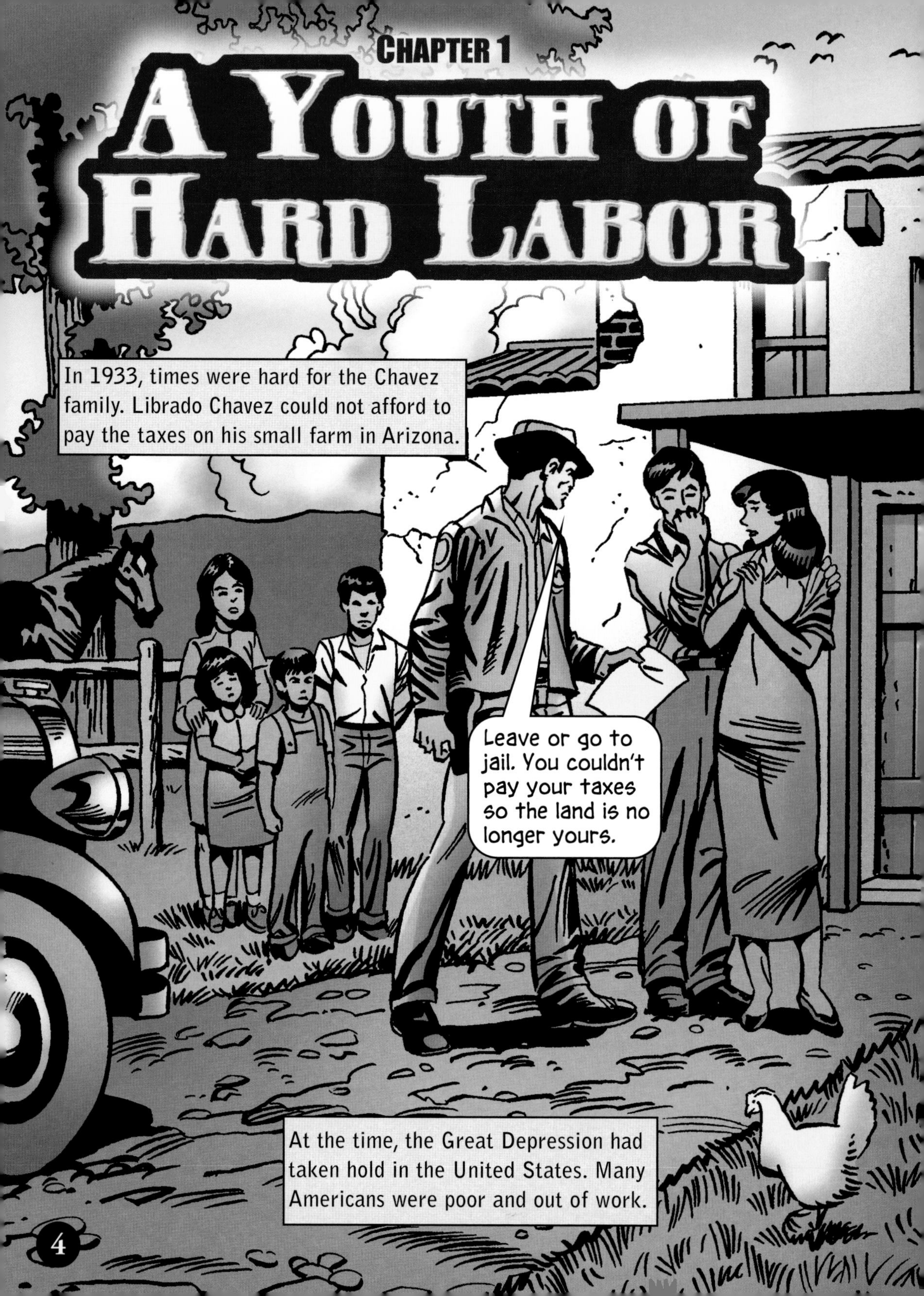
CHAPTER 1
A YOUTH OF HARD LABOR
In 1933, times were hard for the Chavez family. Librado Chavez could not afford to pay the taxes on his small farm in Arizona.
Leave or go to jail. You couldn't pay your taxes so the land is no longer yours.
At the time, the Great Depression had taken hold in the United States. Many Americans were poor and out of work.

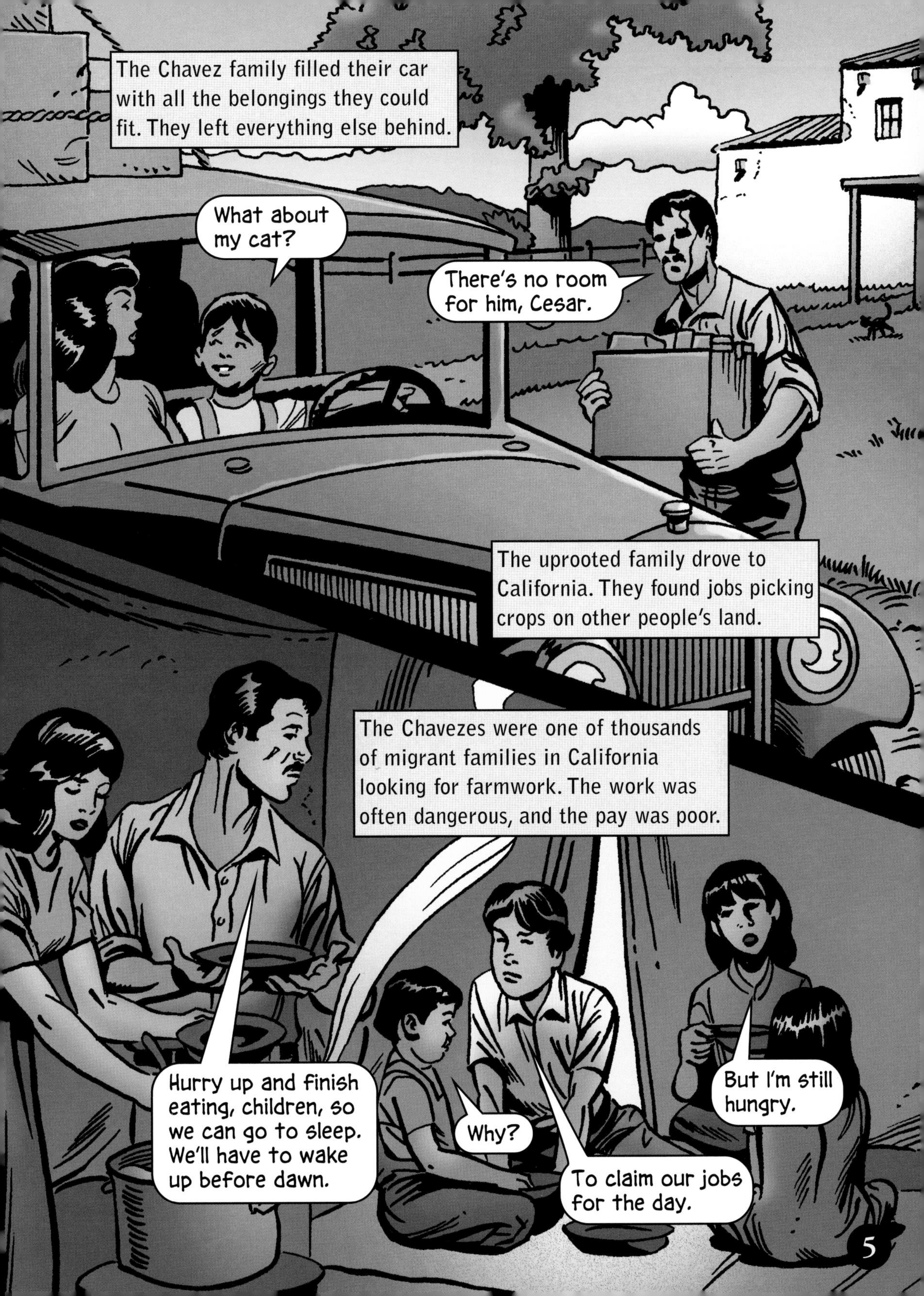
The Chavez family filled their car with all the belongings they could fit. They left everything else behind.
What about my cat?
There's no room for him, Cesar.
The uprooted family drove to California. They found jobs picking crops on other people's land.
The Chavezes were one of thousands of migrant families in California looking for farmwork. The work was often dangerous, and the pay was poor.
Hurry up and finish eating, children, so we can go to sleep. We'll have to wake up before dawn.
Why?
To claim our jobs for the day.
But I'm still hungry.

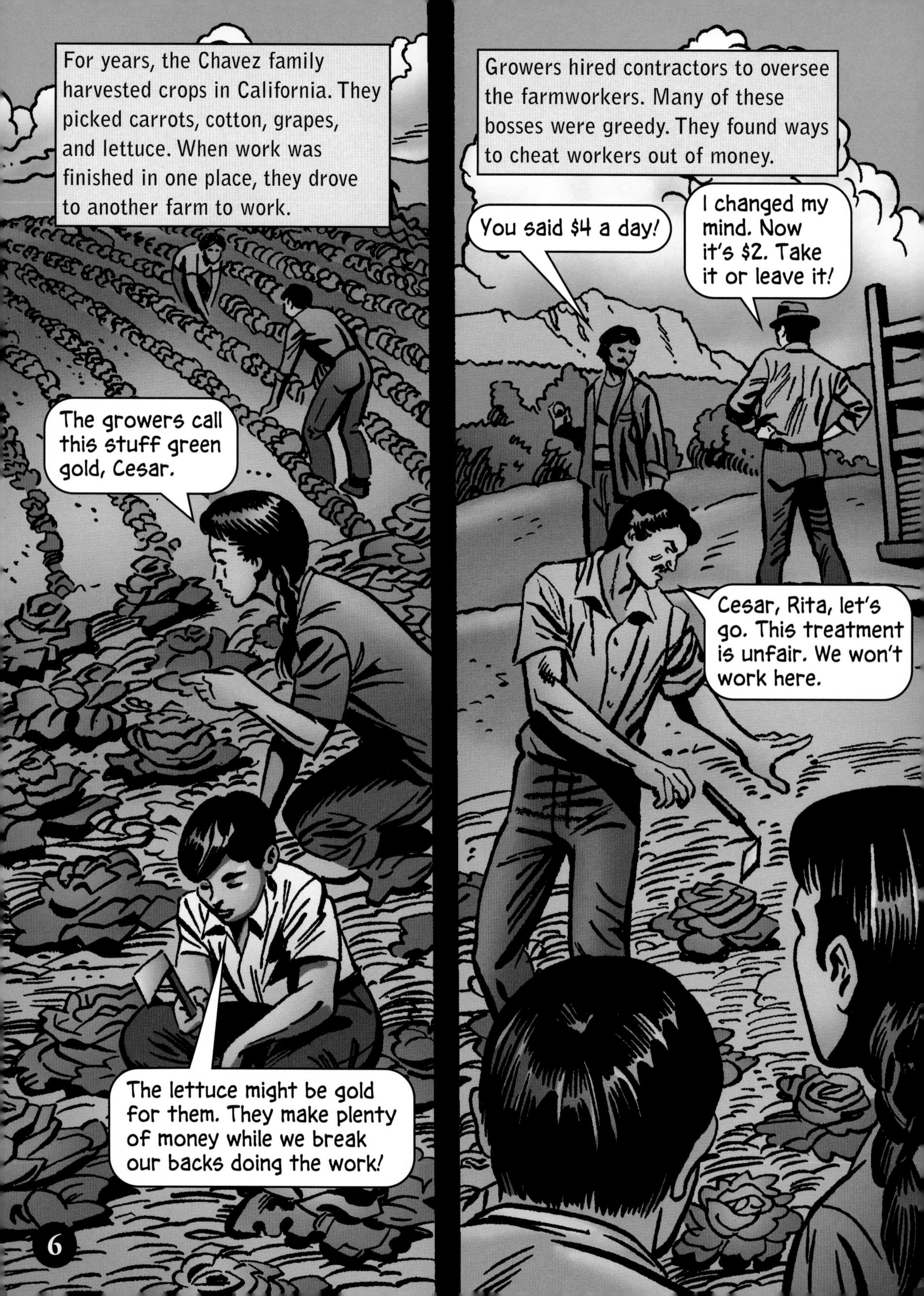
For years, the Chavez family harvested crops in California. They picked carrots, cotton, grapes, and lettuce. When work was finished in one place, they drove to another farm to work.
The growers call this stuff green gold, Cesar.
The lettuce might be gold for them. They make plenty of money while we break our backs doing the work!
Growers hired contractors to oversee the farmworkers. Many of these bosses were greedy. They found ways to cheat workers out of money.
You said $4 a day!
I changed my mind. Now it's $2. Take it or leave it!
Cesar, Rita, let's go. This treatment is unfair. We won't work here.

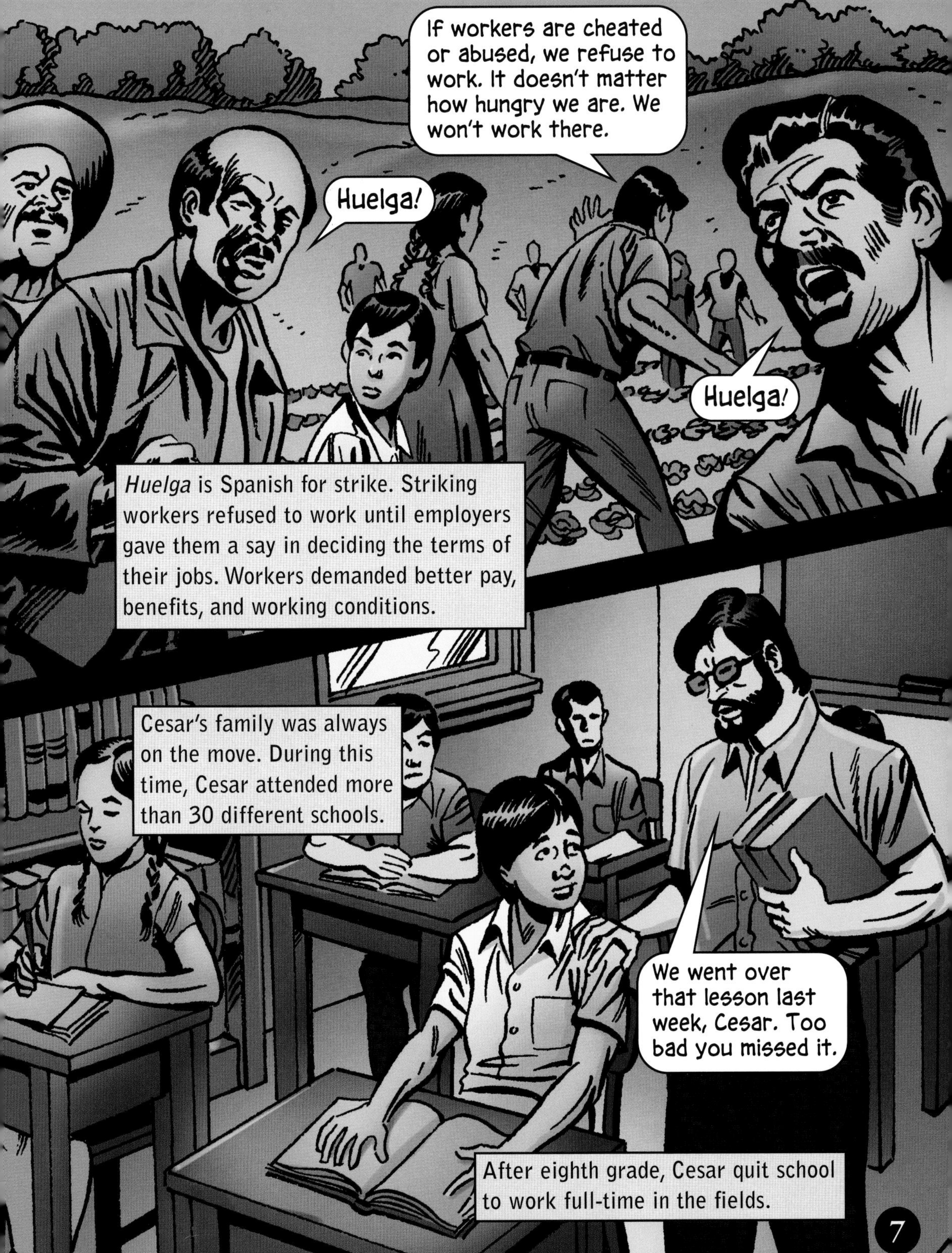
If workers are cheated or abused, we refuse to work. It doesn't matter how hungry we are. We won't work there.
Huelga!
Huelga!
Huelga is Spanish for strike. Striking workers refused to work until employers gave them a say in deciding the terms of their jobs. Workers demanded better pay, benefits, and working conditions.
Cesar's family was always on the move. During this time, Cesar attended more than 30 different schools.
We went over that lesson last week, Cesar. Too bad you missed it.
After eighth grade, Cesar quit school to work full-time in the fields.

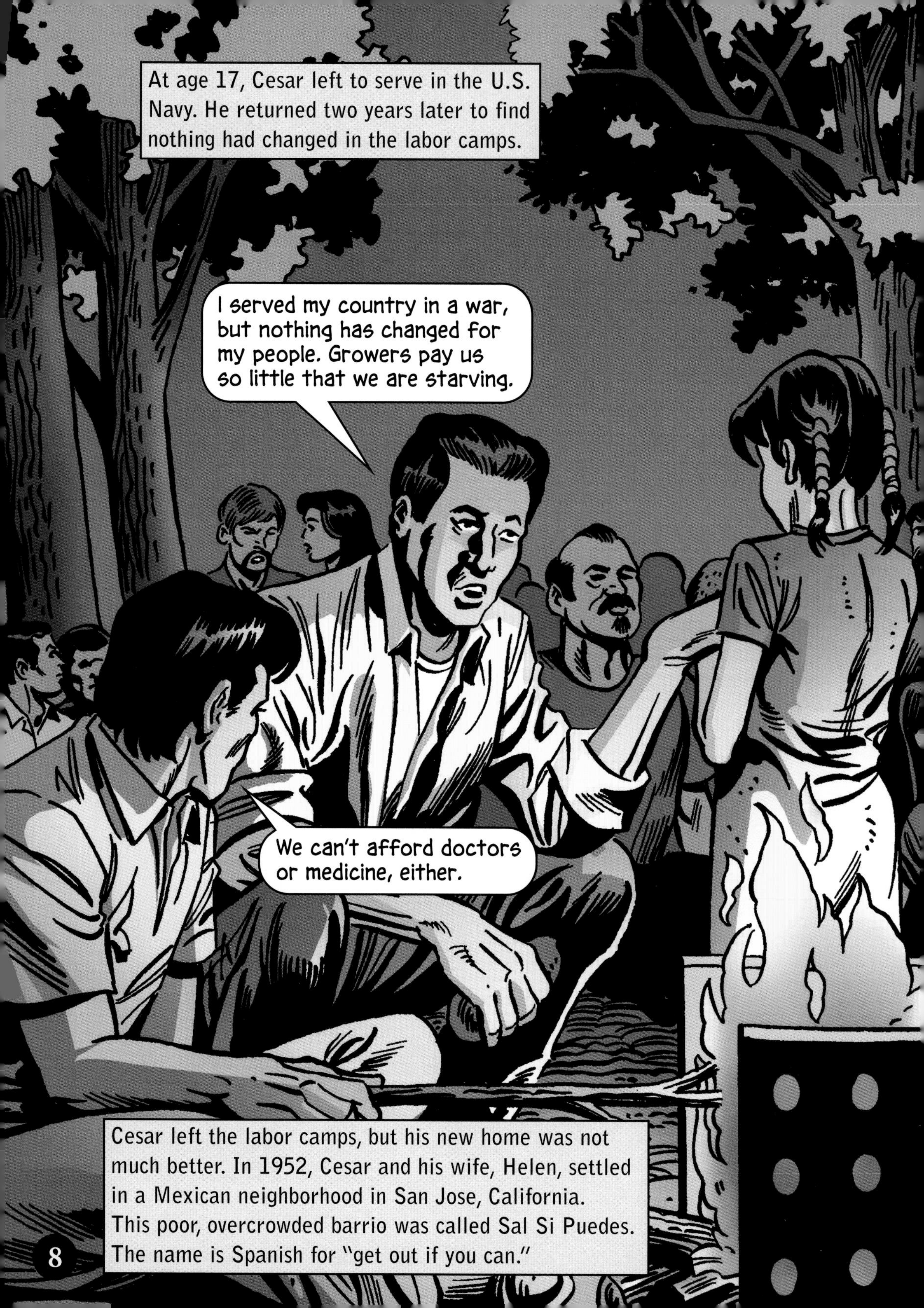
At age 17, Cesar left to serve in the U.S. Navy. He returned two years later to find nothing had changed in the labor camps.
I served my country in a war, but nothing has changed for my people. Growers pay us so little that we are starving.
We can't afford doctors or medicine, either.
Cesar left the labor camps, but his new home was not much better. In 1952, Cesar and his wife, Helen, settled in a Mexican neighborhood in San Jose, California. This poor, overcrowded barrio was called Sal Si Puedes. The name is Spanish for "get out if you can."

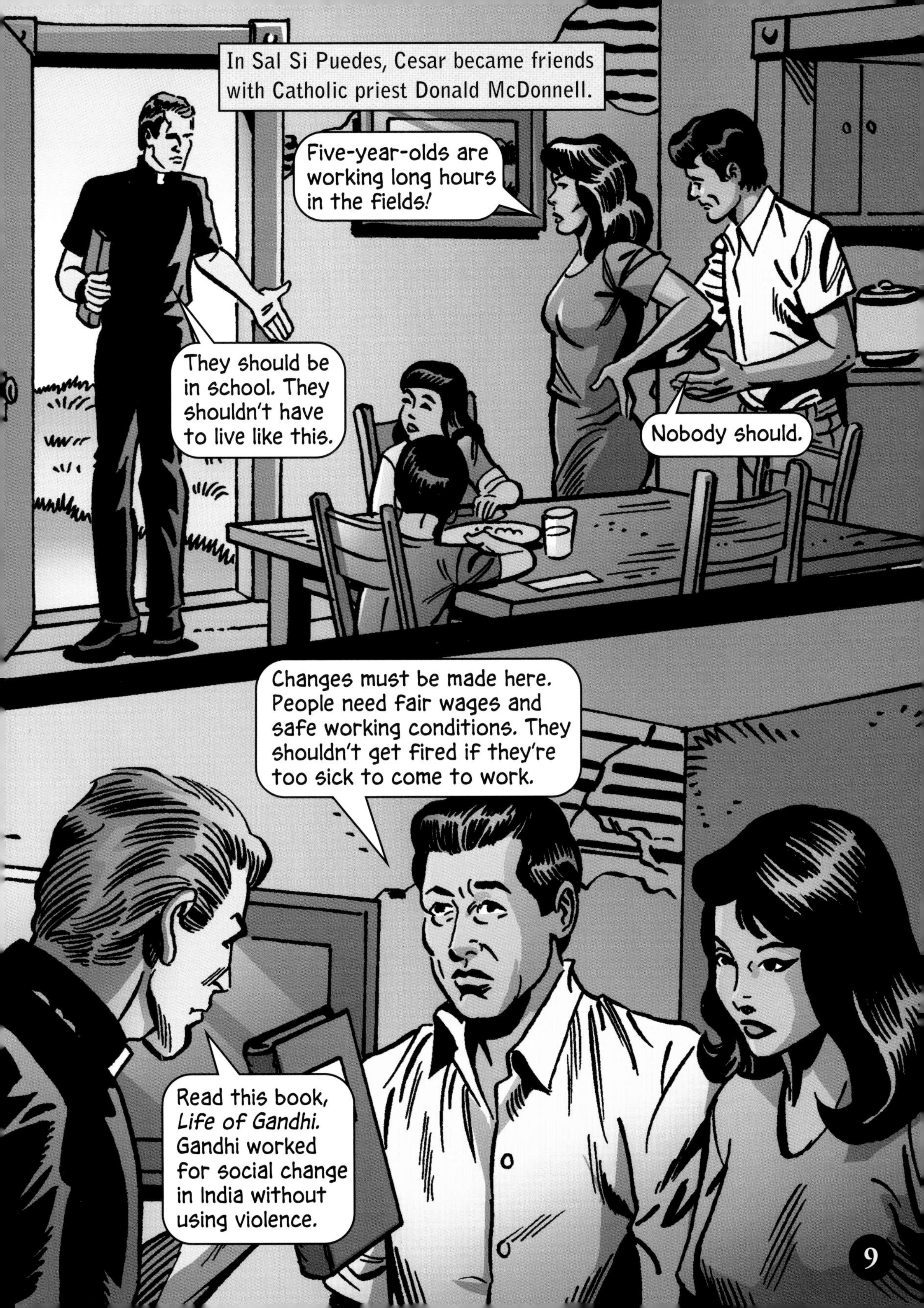
In Sal Si Puedes, Cesar became friends with Catholic priest Donald McDonnell.
Five-year-olds are working long hours in the fields!
They should be in school. They shouldn't have to live like this.
Nobody should.
Changes must be made here. People need fair wages and safe working conditions. They shouldn't get fired if they're too sick to come to work.
Read this book, *Life of Gandhi.* Gandhi worked for social change in India without using violence.

CHAPTER 2

GETTING ORGANIZED

In June 1952, an Anglo stranger named Fred Ross came to Cesar's home. Ross worked for a Latino civil rights group called the Community Service Organization (CSO). At first, Cesar and his friends didn't trust Ross.

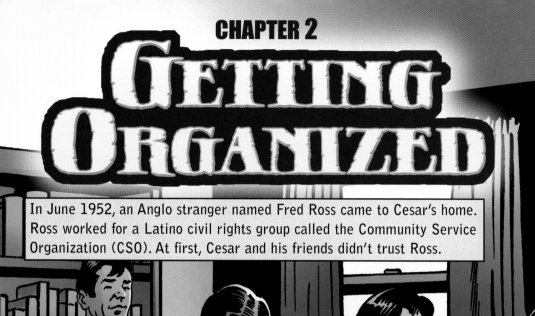

The creek your kids play in is dirty. The cops beat you up. Your paychecks are tiny.

He seems to understand our problems.

What will you do about it?

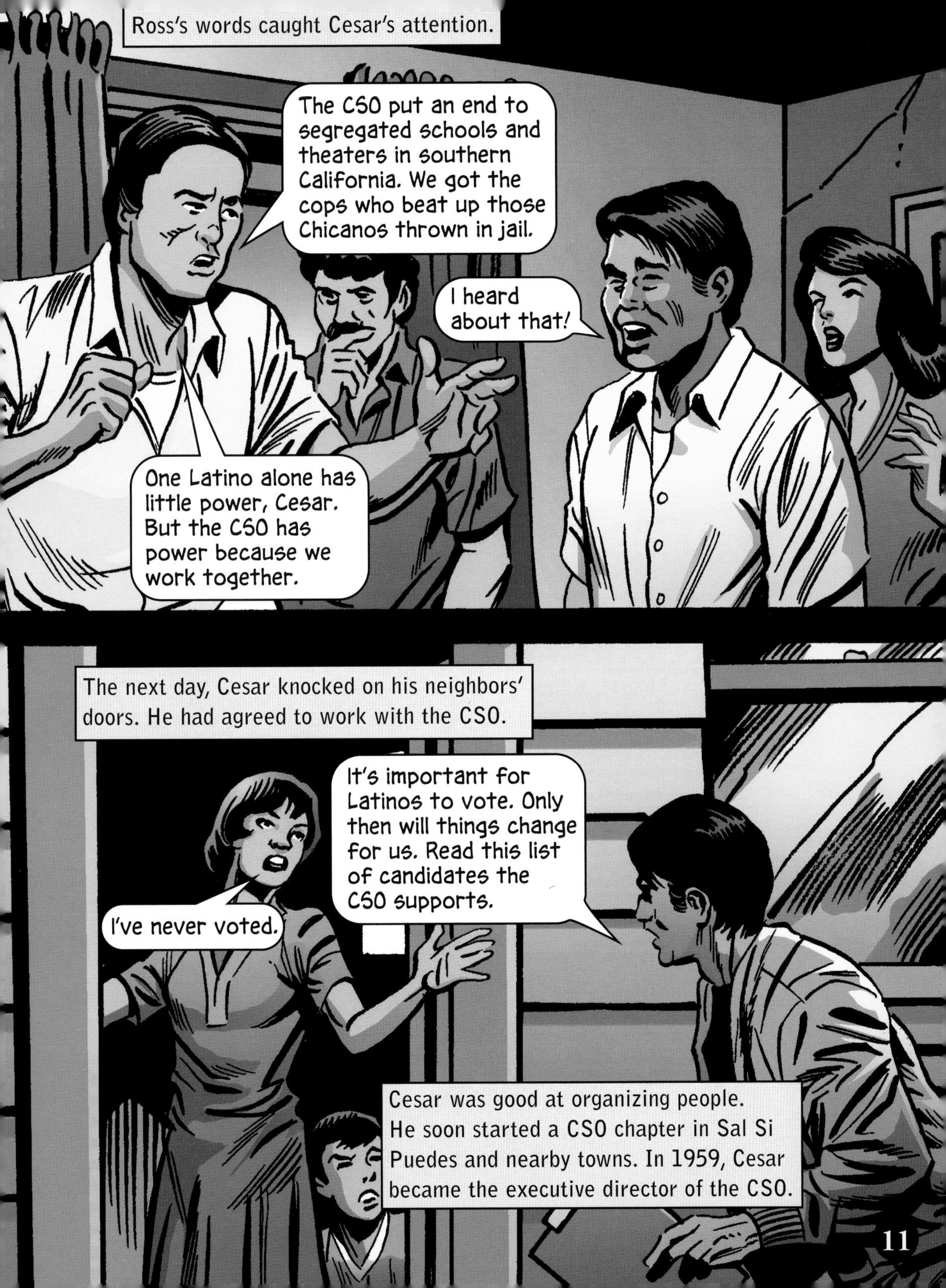
Ross's words caught Cesar's attention.
The CSO put an end to segregated schools and theaters in southern California. We got the cops who beat up those Chicanos thrown in jail.
I heard about that!
One Latino alone has little power, Cesar. But the CSO has power because we work together.
The next day, Cesar knocked on his neighbors' doors. He had agreed to work with the CSO.
It's important for Latinos to vote. Only then will things change for us. Read this list of candidates the CSO supports.
I've never voted.
Cesar was good at organizing people. He soon started a CSO chapter in Sal Si Puedes and nearby towns. In 1959, Cesar became the executive director of the CSO.

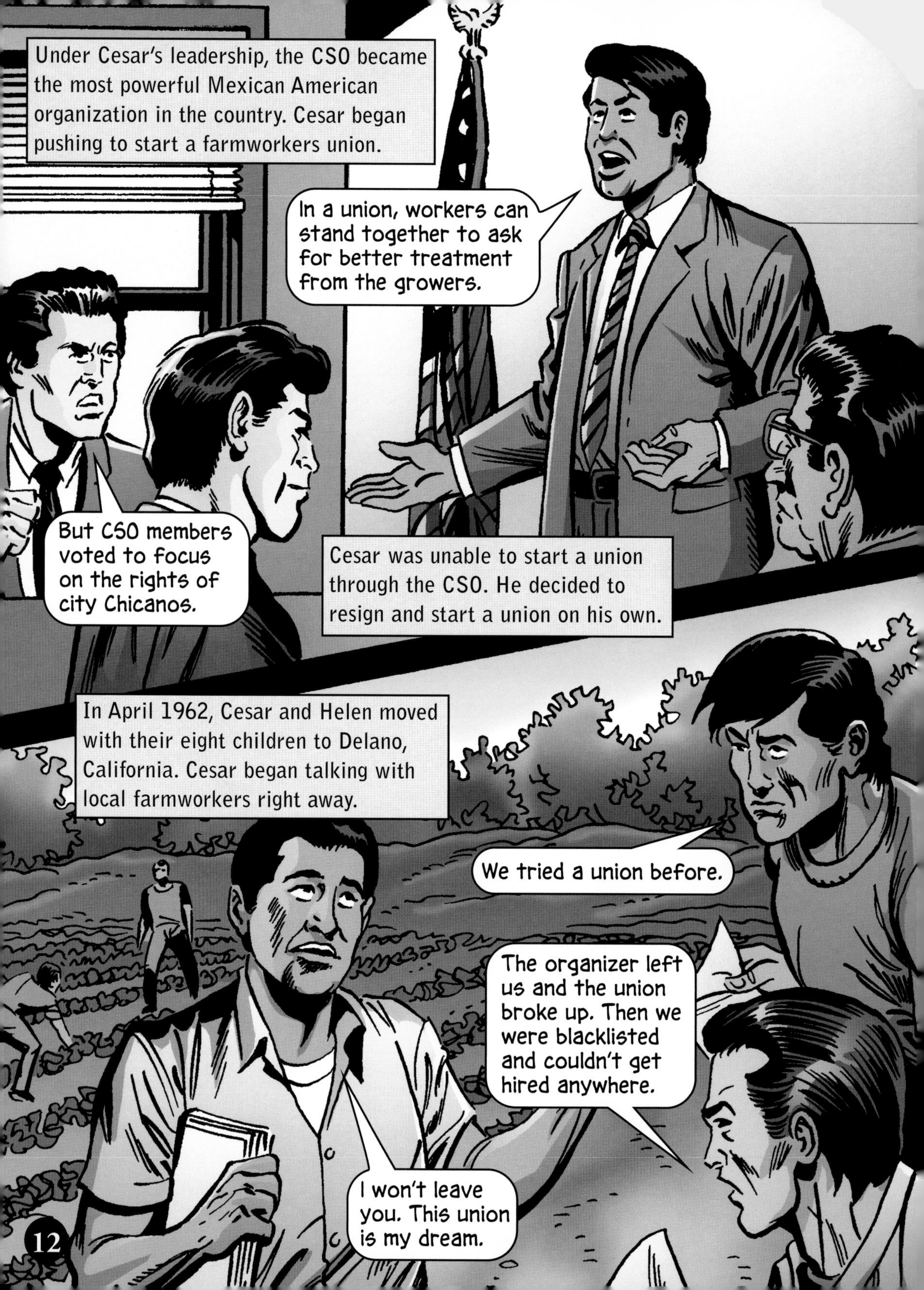

Under Cesar's leadership, the CSO became the most powerful Mexican American organization in the country. Cesar began pushing to start a farmworkers union.
In a union, workers can stand together to ask for better treatment from the growers.
But CSO members voted to focus on the rights of city Chicanos.
Cesar was unable to start a union through the CSO. He decided to resign and start a union on his own.
In April 1962, Cesar and Helen moved with their eight children to Delano, California. Cesar began talking with local farmworkers right away.
We tried a union before.
The organizer left us and the union broke up. Then we were blacklisted and couldn't get hired anywhere.
I won't leave you. This union is my dream.

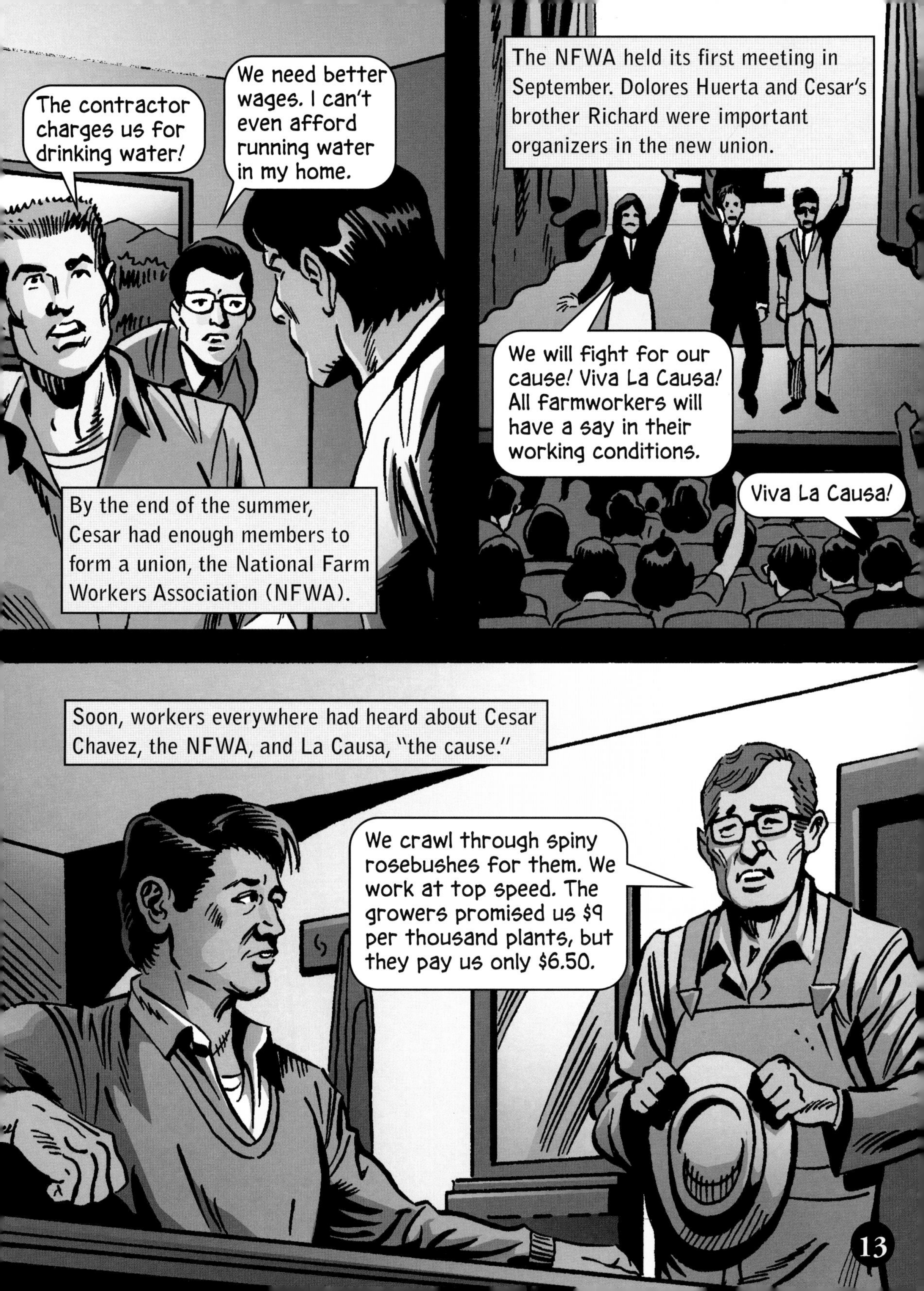

The contractor charges us for drinking water!
We need better wages. I can't even afford running water in my home.
By the end of the summer, Cesar had enough members to form a union, the National Farm Workers Association (NFWA).
The NFWA held its first meeting in September. Dolores Huerta and Cesar's brother Richard were important organizers in the new union.
We will fight for our cause! Viva La Causa! All farmworkers will have a say in their working conditions.
Viva La Causa!
Soon, workers everywhere had heard about Cesar Chavez, the NFWA, and La Causa, "the cause."
We crawl through spiny rosebushes for them. We work at top speed. The growers promised us $9 per thousand plants, but they pay us only $6.50.

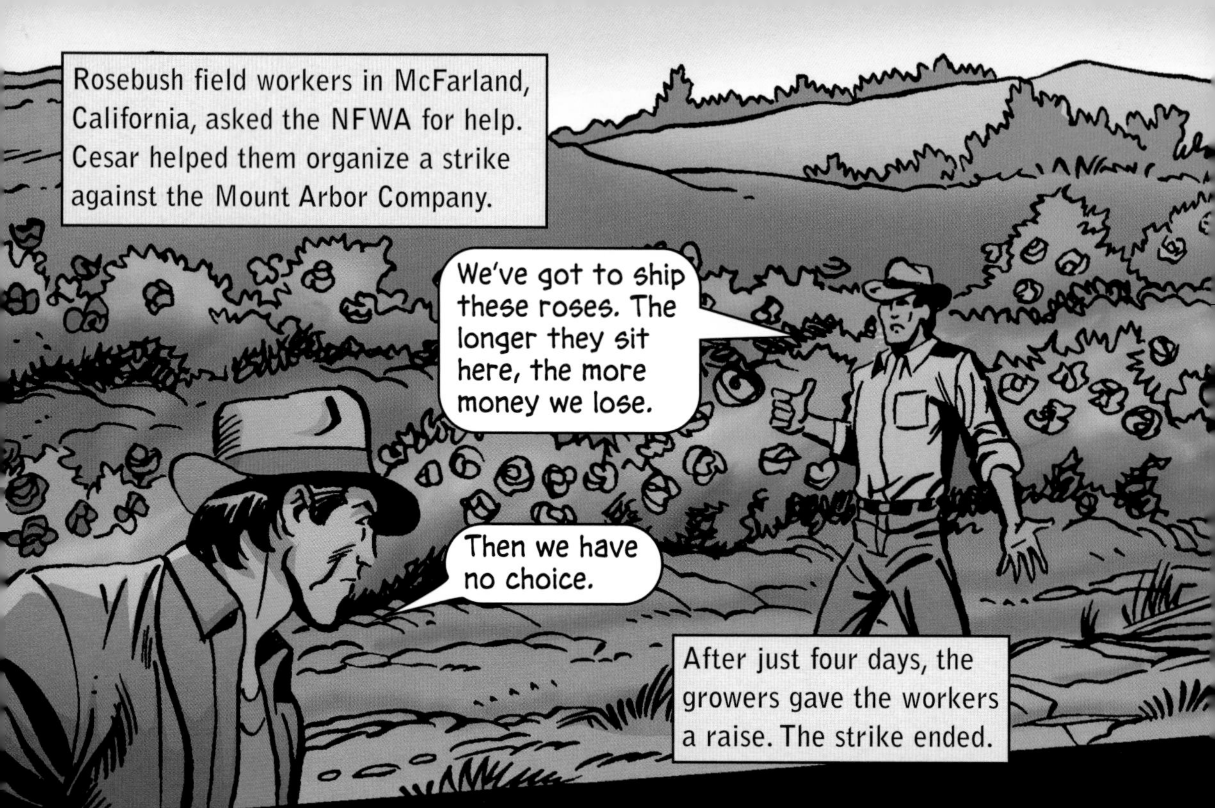
Rosebush field workers in McFarland, California, asked the NFWA for help. Cesar helped them organize a strike against the Mount Arbor Company.
We've got to ship these roses. The longer they sit here, the more money we lose.
Then we have no choice.
After just four days, the growers gave the workers a raise. The strike ended.

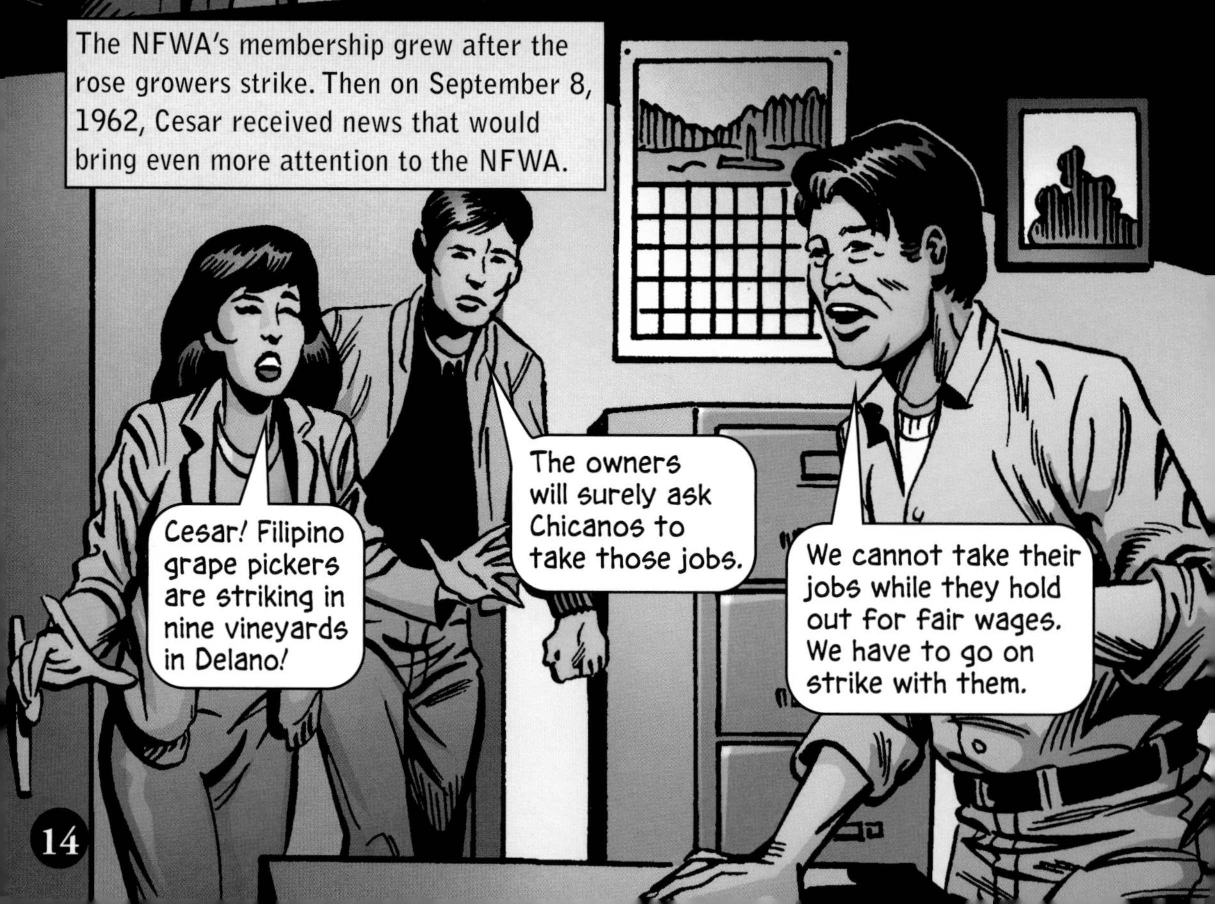
The NFWA's membership grew after the rose growers strike. Then on September 8, 1962, Cesar received news that would bring even more attention to the NFWA.
Cesar! Filipino grape pickers are striking in nine vineyards in Delano!
The owners will surely ask Chicanos to take those jobs.
We cannot take their jobs while they hold out for fair wages. We have to go on strike with them.

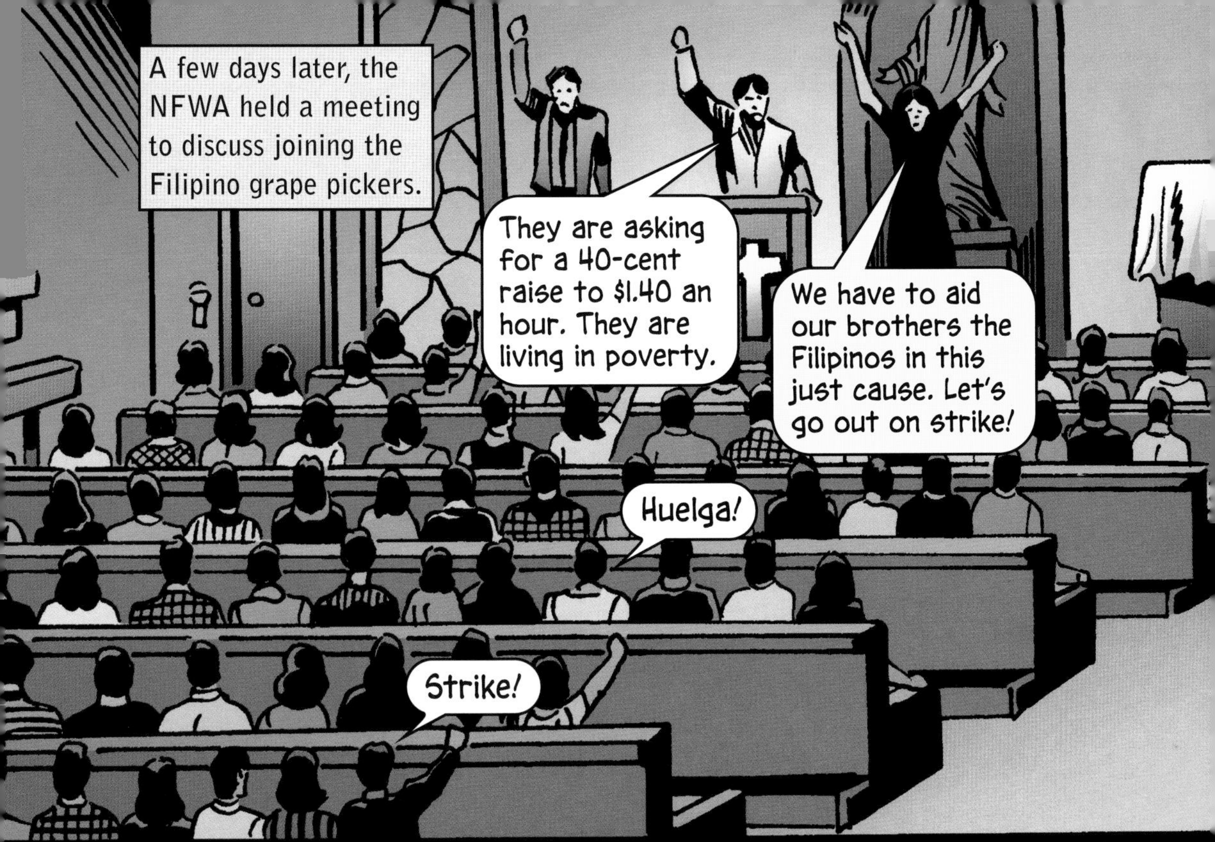
A few days later, the NFWA held a meeting to discuss joining the Filipino grape pickers.
They are asking for a 40-cent raise to $1.40 an hour. They are living in poverty.
We have to aid our brothers the Filipinos in this just cause. Let's go out on strike!
Huelga!
Strike!

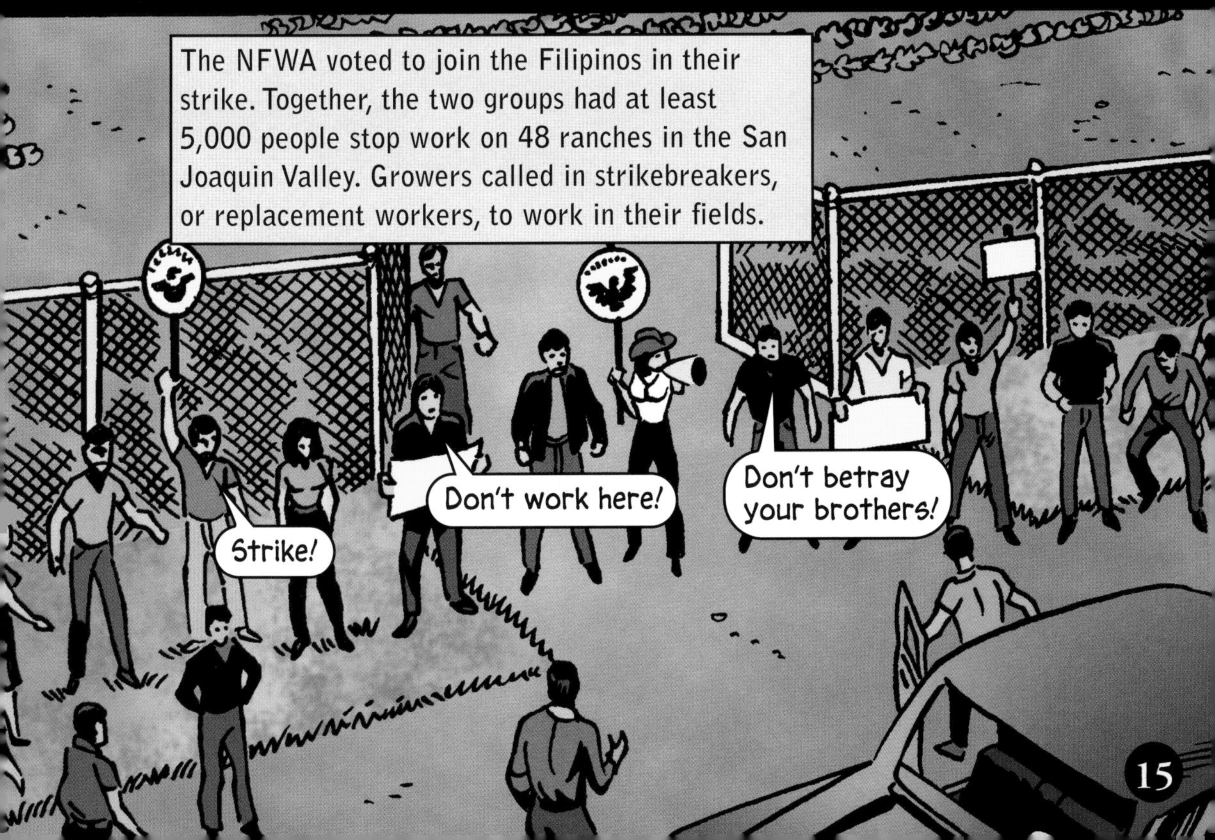
The NFWA voted to join the Filipinos in their strike. Together, the two groups had at least 5,000 people stop work on 48 ranches in the San Joaquin Valley. Growers called in strikebreakers, or replacement workers, to work in their fields.
Strike!
Don't work here!
Don't betray your brothers!

CHAPTER 3

The Great Delano Grape Strike

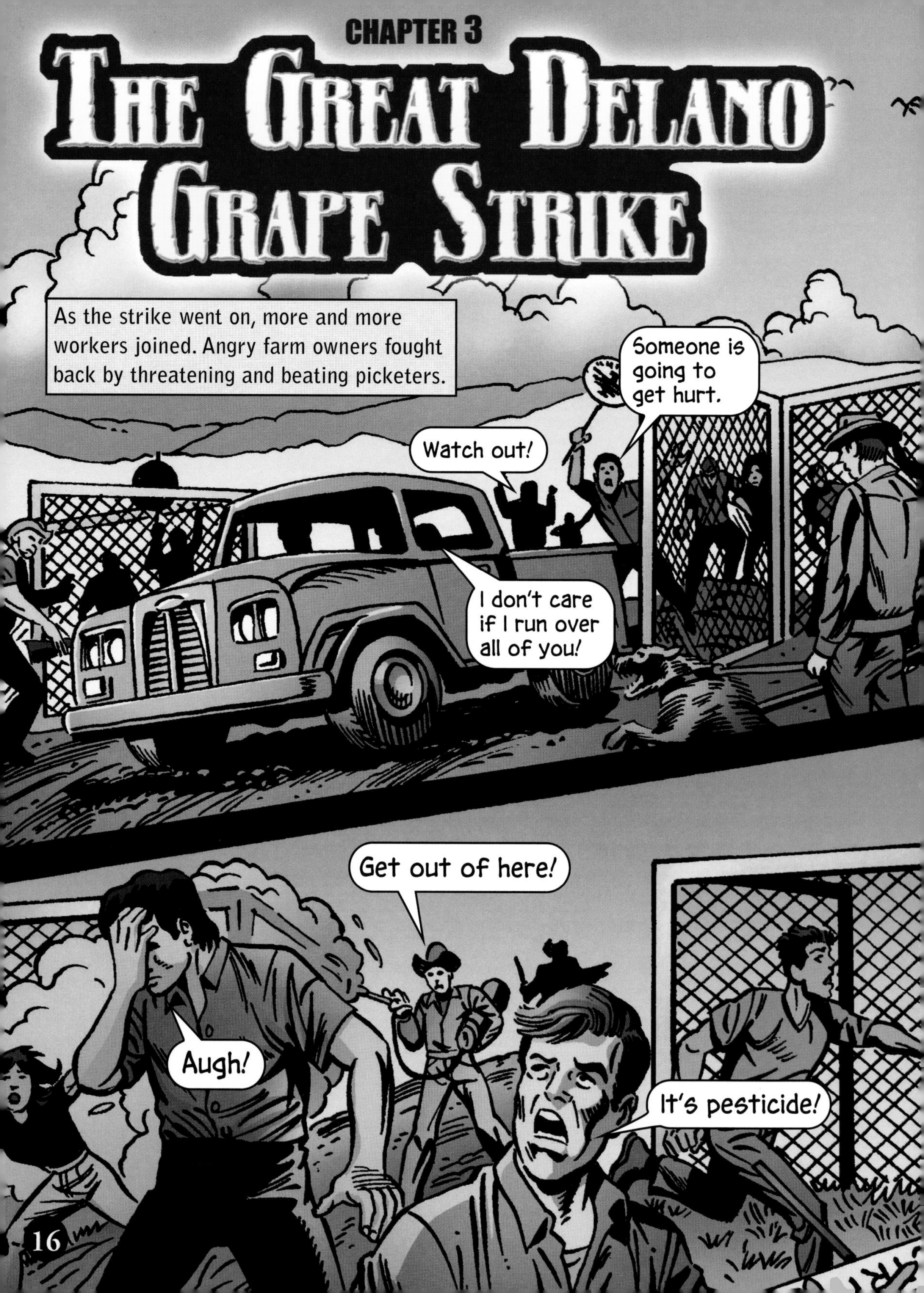

As the strike went on, more and more workers joined. Angry farm owners fought back by threatening and beating picketers.
Watch out!
Someone is going to get hurt.
I don't care if I run over all of you!
Get out of here!
Augh!
It's pesticide!

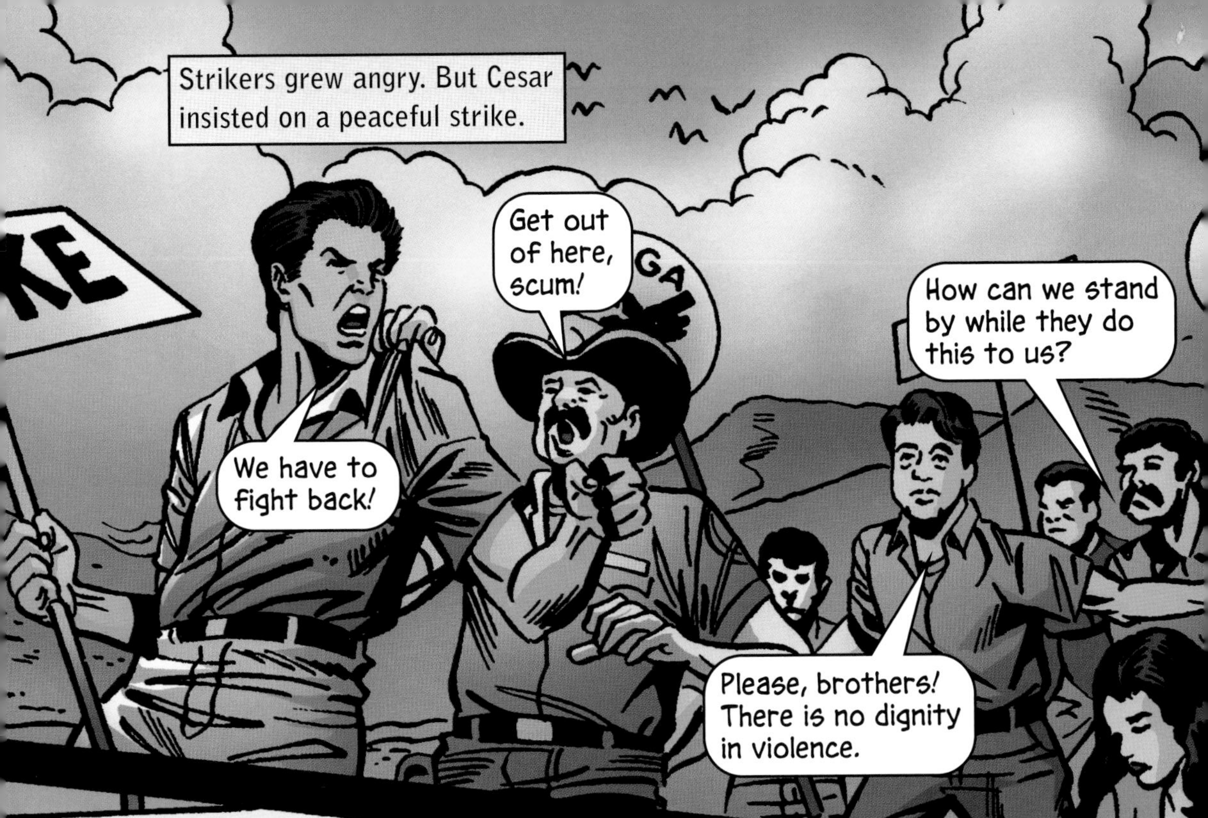
Strikers grew angry. But Cesar insisted on a peaceful strike.
We have to fight back!
Get out of here, scum!
How can we stand by while they do this to us?
Please, brothers! There is no dignity in violence.

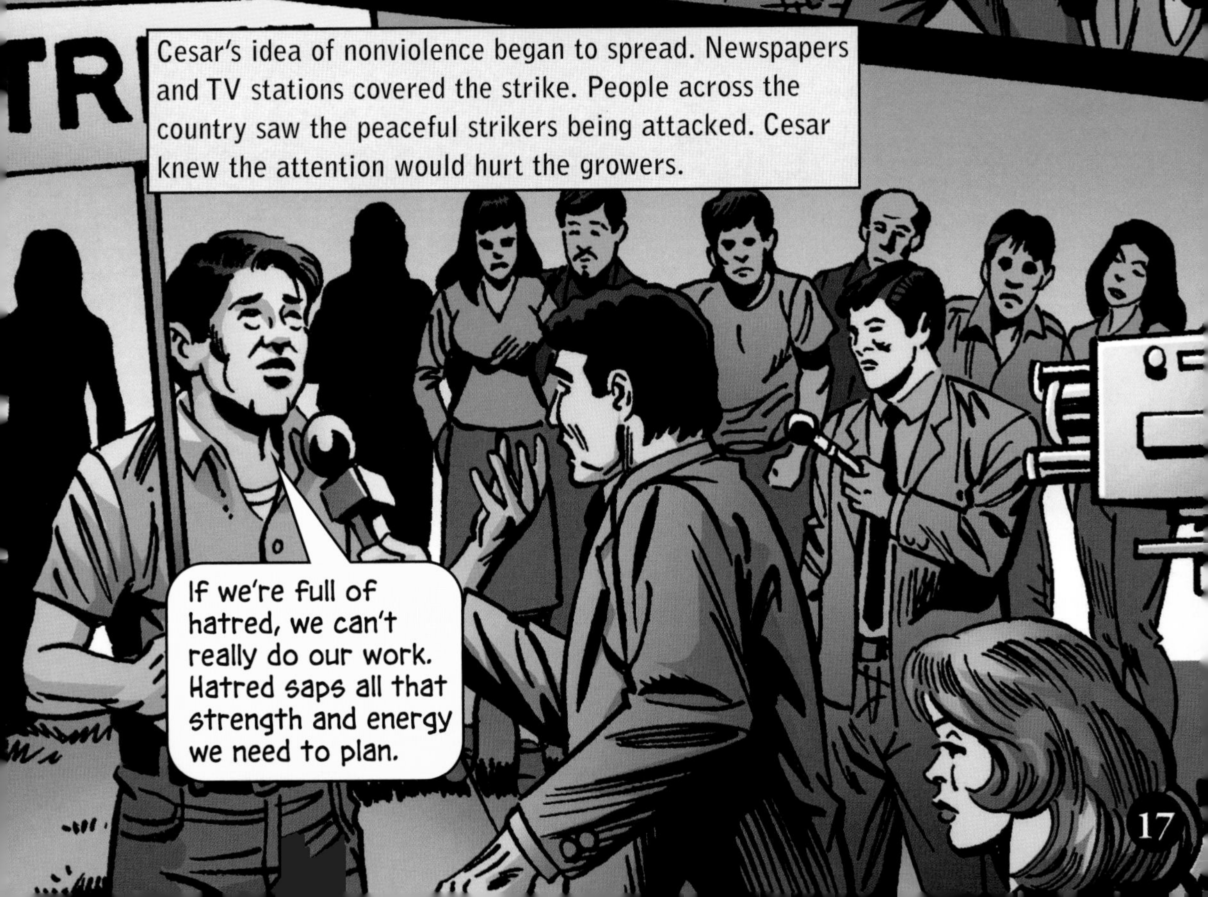
Cesar's idea of nonviolence began to spread. Newspapers and TV stations covered the strike. People across the country saw the peaceful strikers being attacked. Cesar knew the attention would hurt the growers.
If we're full of hatred, we can't really do our work. Hatred saps all that strength and energy we need to plan.

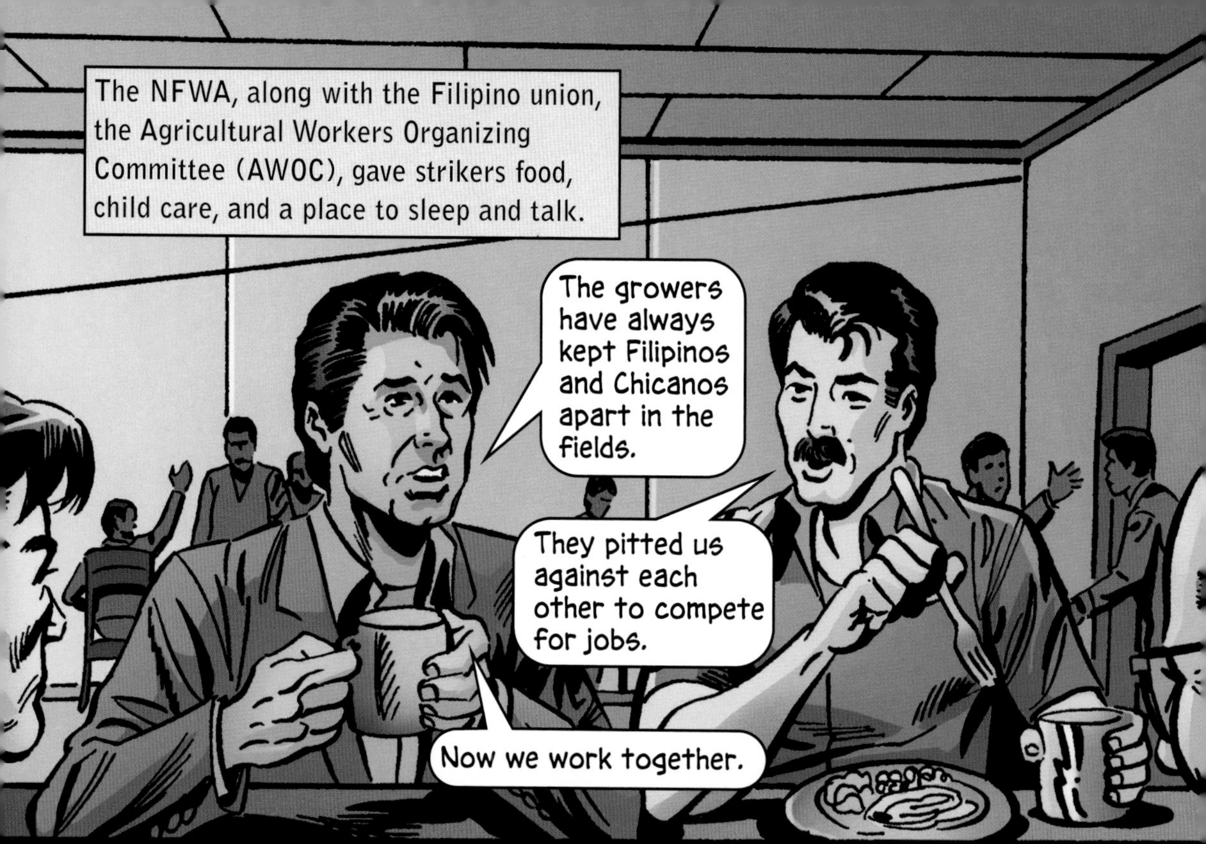
The NFWA, along with the Filipino union, the Agricultural Workers Organizing Committee (AWOC), gave strikers food, child care, and a place to sleep and talk.
The growers have always kept Filipinos and Chicanos apart in the fields.
They pitted us against each other to compete for jobs.
Now we work together.

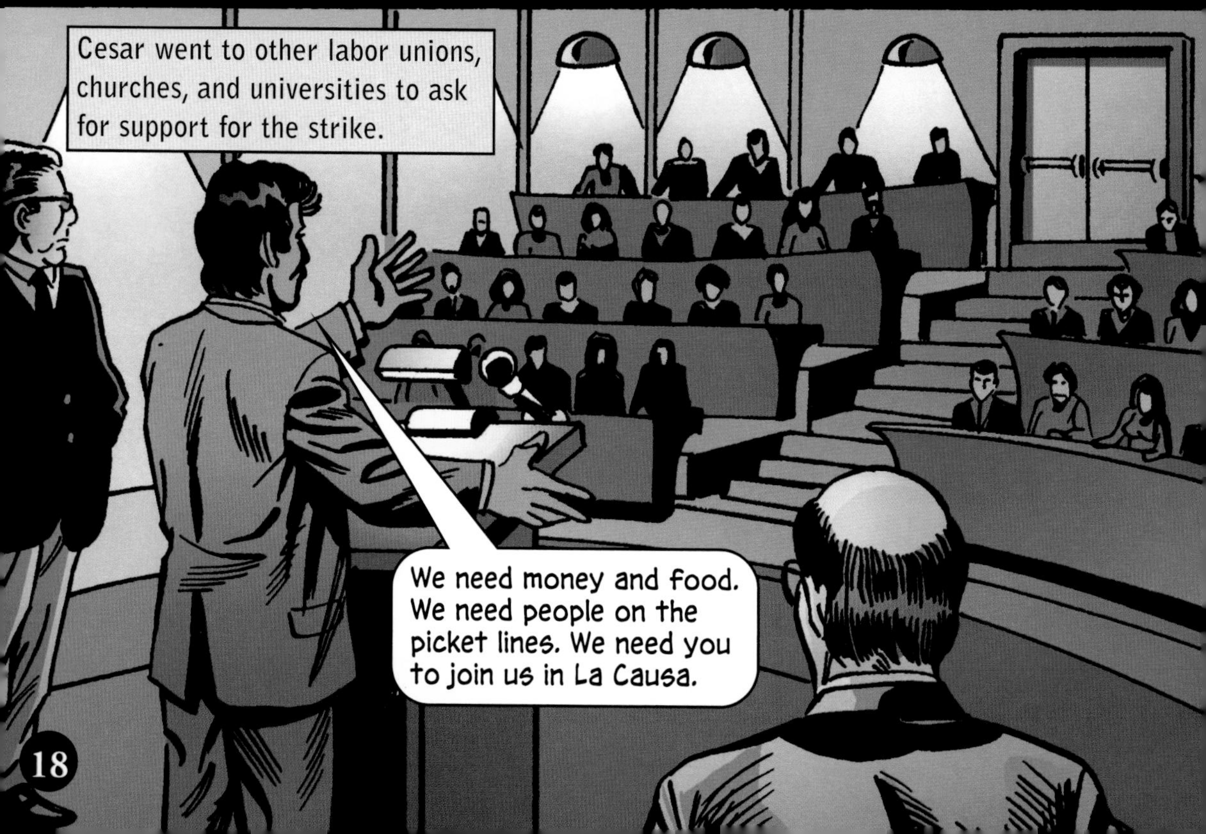
Cesar went to other labor unions, churches, and universities to ask for support for the strike.
We need money and food. We need people on the picket lines. We need you to join us in La Causa.

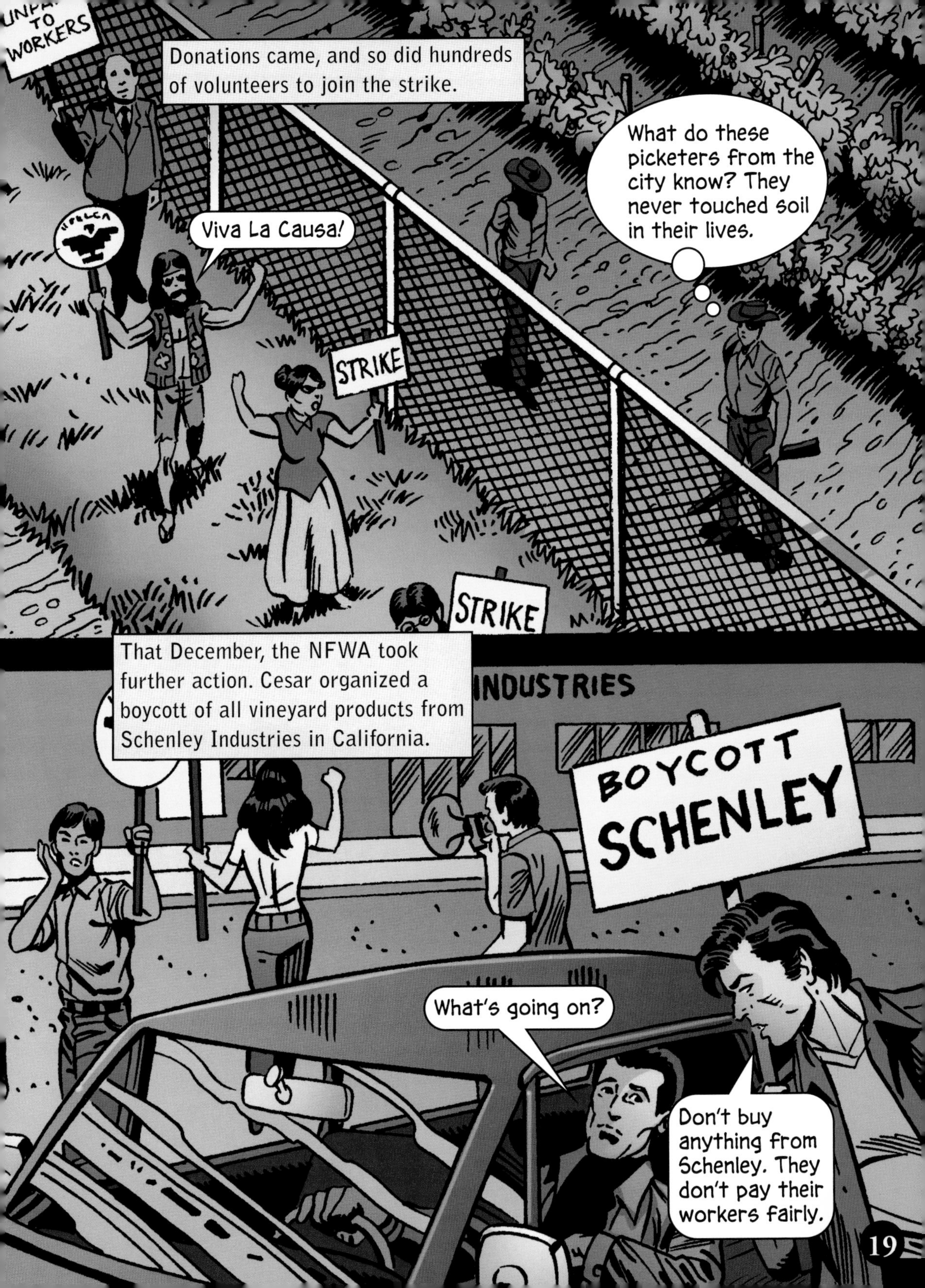
TO WORKERS
Donations came, and so did hundreds of volunteers to join the strike.
Viva La Causa!
What do these picketers from the city know? They never touched soil in their lives.
STRIKE
STRIKE
That December, the NFWA took further action. Cesar organized a boycott of all vineyard products from Schenley Industries in California.
INDUSTRIES
BOYCOTT SCHENLEY
What's going on?
Don't buy anything from Schenley. They don't pay their workers fairly.

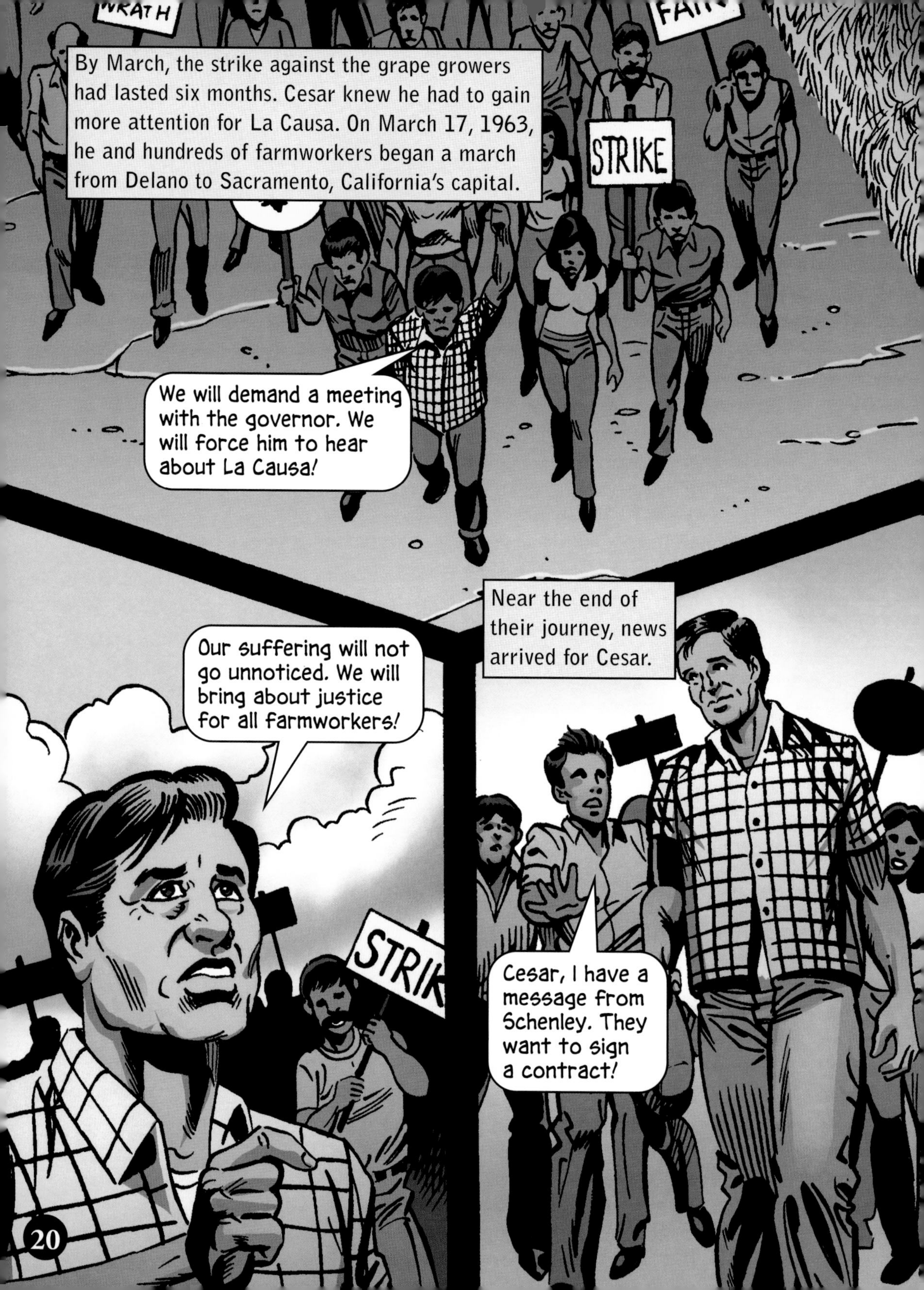
By March, the strike against the grape growers had lasted six months. Cesar knew he had to gain more attention for La Causa. On March 17, 1963, he and hundreds of farmworkers began a march from Delano to Sacramento, California's capital.
STRIKE
We will demand a meeting with the governor. We will force him to hear about La Causa!
Our suffering will not go unnoticed. We will bring about justice for all farmworkers!
Near the end of their journey, news arrived for Cesar.
Cesar, I have a message from Schenley. They want to sign a contract!

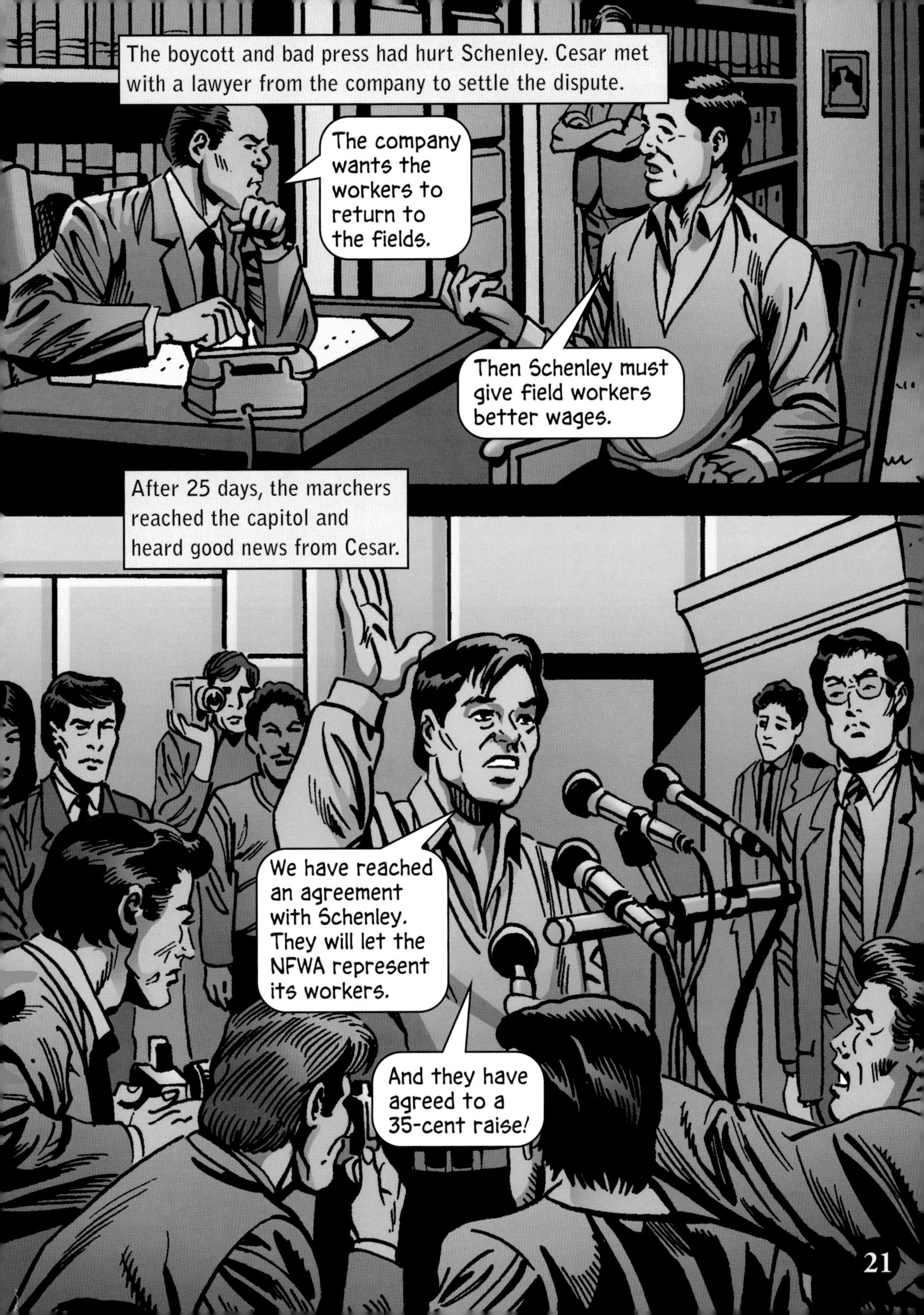
The boycott and bad press had hurt Schenley. Cesar met with a lawyer from the company to settle the dispute.
The company wants the workers to return to the fields.
Then Schenley must give field workers better wages.
After 25 days, the marchers reached the capitol and heard good news from Cesar.
We have reached an agreement with Schenley. They will let the NFWA represent its workers.
And they have agreed to a 35-cent raise!

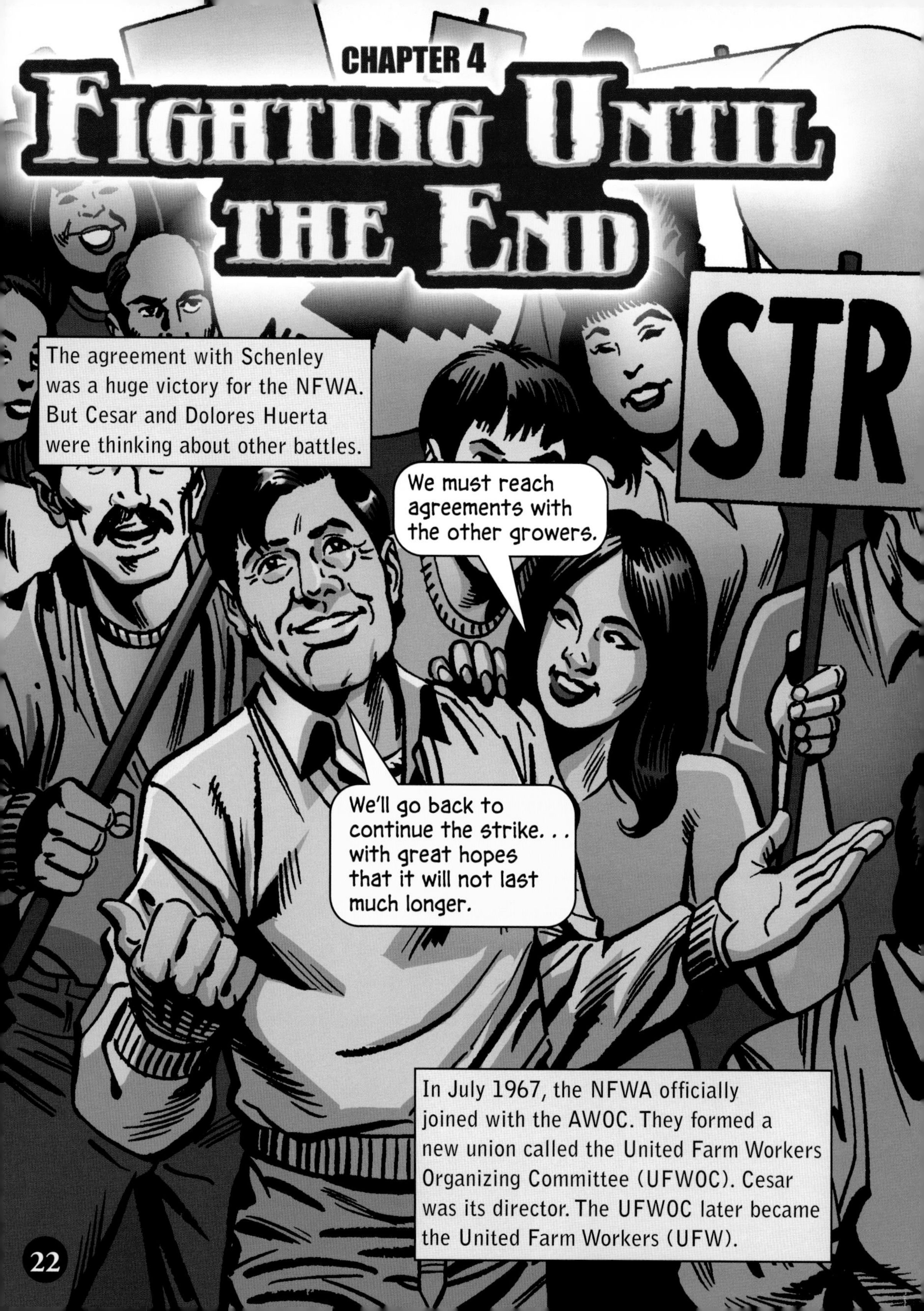
CHAPTER 4
FIGHTING UNTIL THE END
The agreement with Schenley was a huge victory for the NFWA. But Cesar and Dolores Huerta were thinking about other battles.
STR
We must reach agreements with the other growers.
We'll go back to continue the strike. . . with great hopes that it will not last much longer.
In July 1967, the NFWA officially joined with the AWOC. They formed a new union called the United Farm Workers Organizing Committee (UFWOC). Cesar was its director. The UFWOC later became the United Farm Workers (UFW).

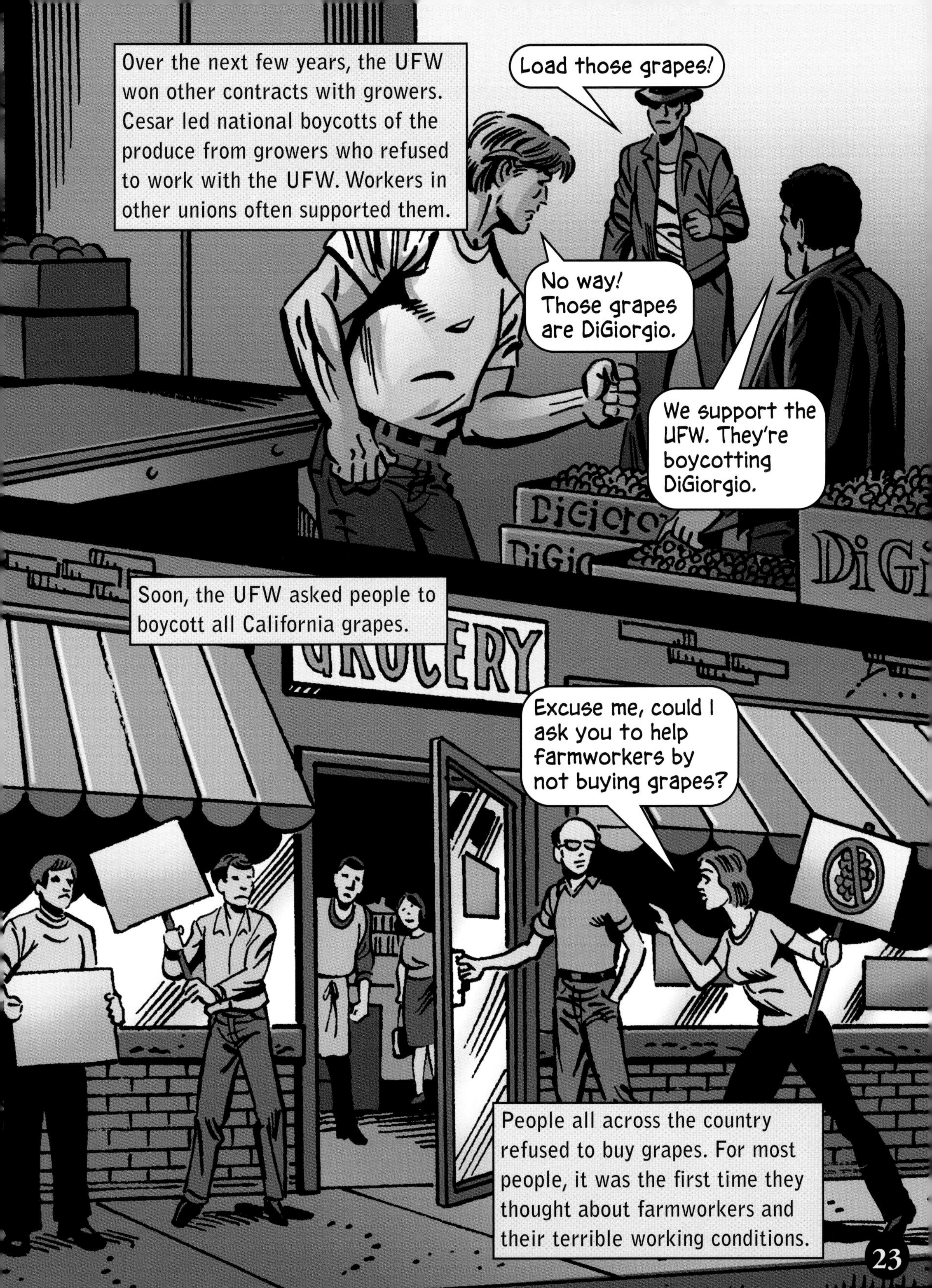
Over the next few years, the UFW won other contracts with growers. Cesar led national boycotts of the produce from growers who refused to work with the UFW. Workers in other unions often supported them.
Load those grapes!
No way! Those grapes are DiGiorgio.
We support the UFW. They're boycotting DiGiorgio.
Soon, the UFW asked people to boycott all California grapes.
Excuse me, could I ask you to help farmworkers by not buying grapes?
People all across the country refused to buy grapes. For most people, it was the first time they thought about farmworkers and their terrible working conditions.

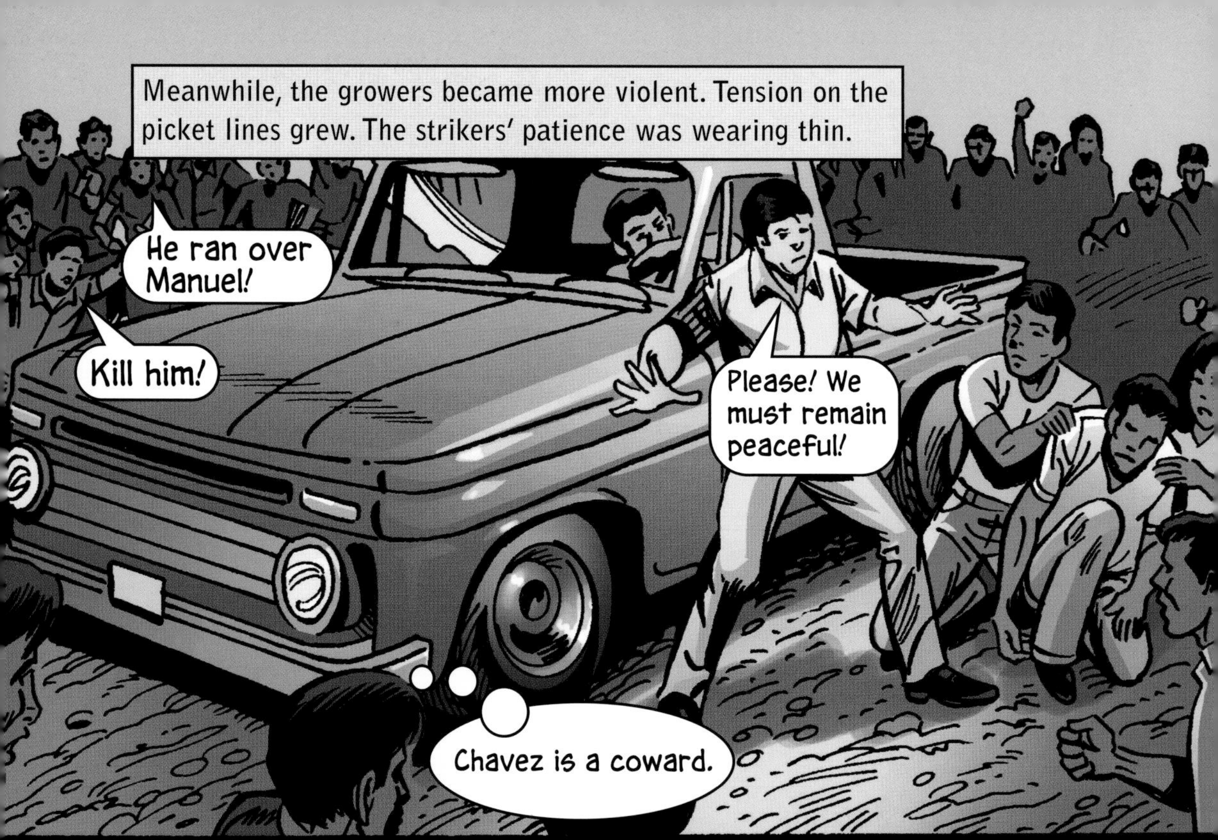
Meanwhile, the growers became more violent. Tension on the picket lines grew. The strikers' patience was wearing thin.
He ran over Manuel!
Kill him!
Please! We must remain peaceful!
Chavez is a coward.

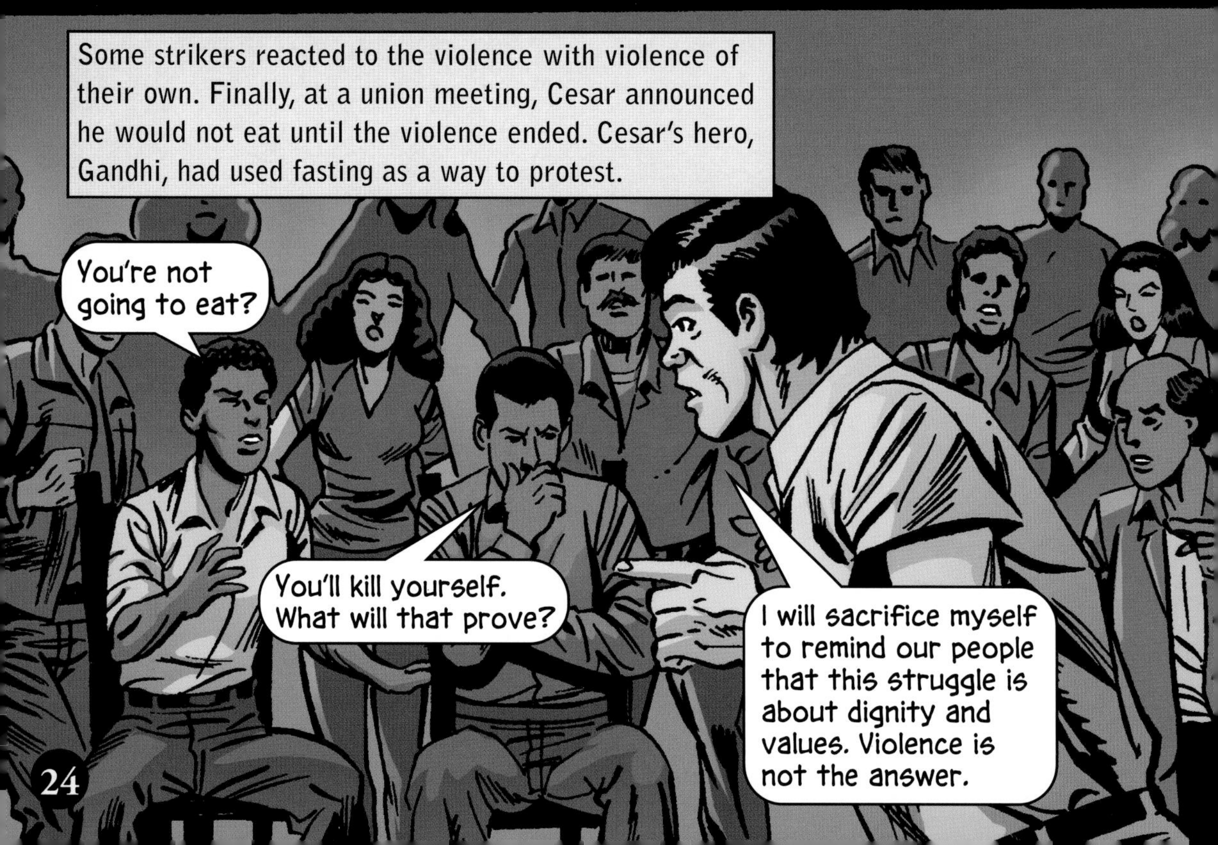
Some strikers reacted to the violence with violence of their own. Finally, at a union meeting, Cesar announced he would not eat until the violence ended. Cesar's hero, Gandhi, had used fasting as a way to protest.
You're not going to eat?
You'll kill yourself. What will that prove?
I will sacrifice myself to remind our people that this struggle is about dignity and values. Violence is not the answer.

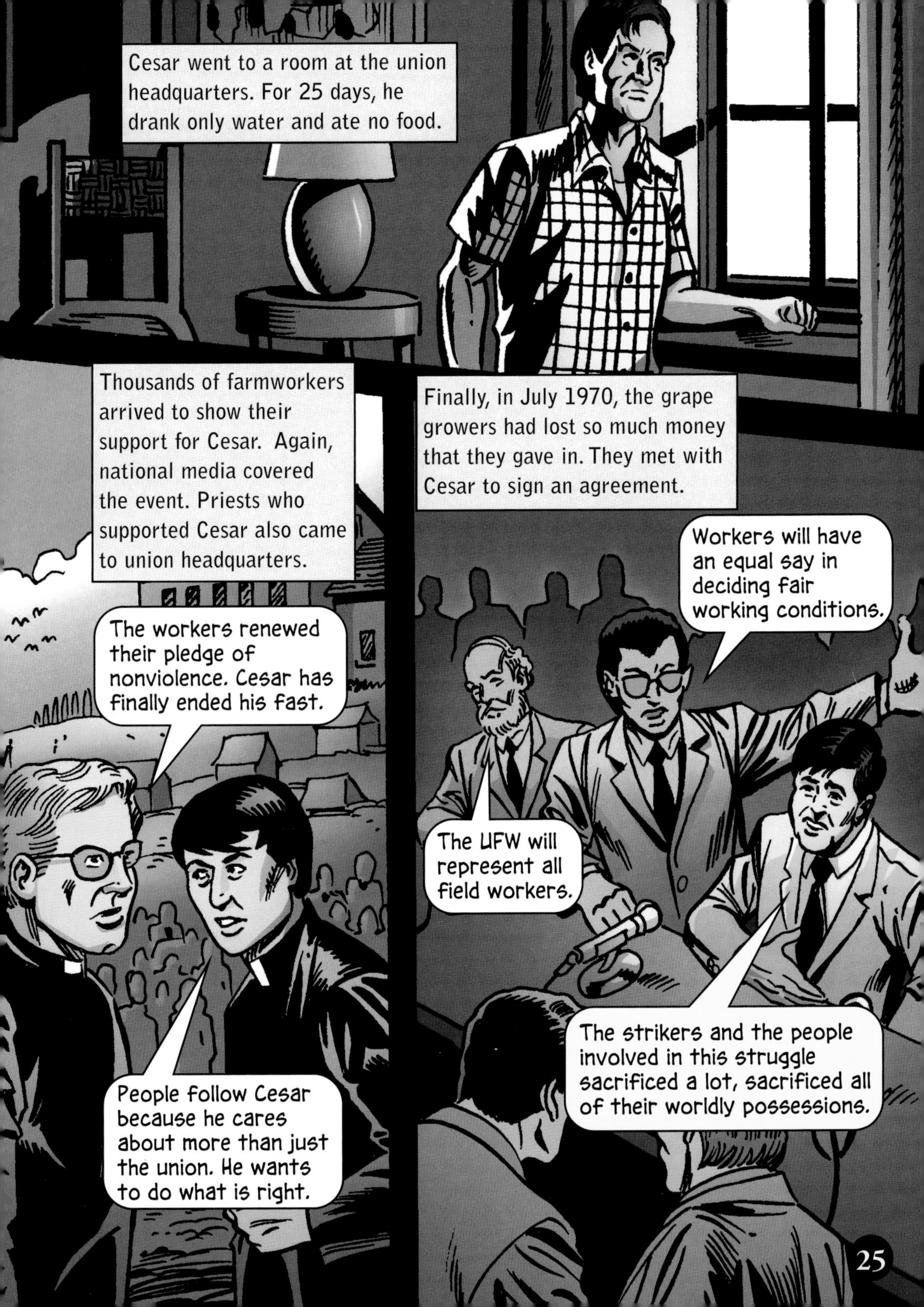

Cesar went to a room at the union headquarters. For 25 days, he drank only water and ate no food.
Thousands of farmworkers arrived to show their support for Cesar. Again, national media covered the event. Priests who supported Cesar also came to union headquarters.
The workers renewed their pledge of nonviolence. Cesar has finally ended his fast.
People follow Cesar because he cares about more than just the union. He wants to do what is right.
Finally, in July 1970, the grape growers had lost so much money that they gave in. They met with Cesar to sign an agreement.
Workers will have an equal say in deciding fair working conditions.
The UFW will represent all field workers.
The strikers and the people involved in this struggle sacrificed a lot, sacrificed all of their worldly possessions.

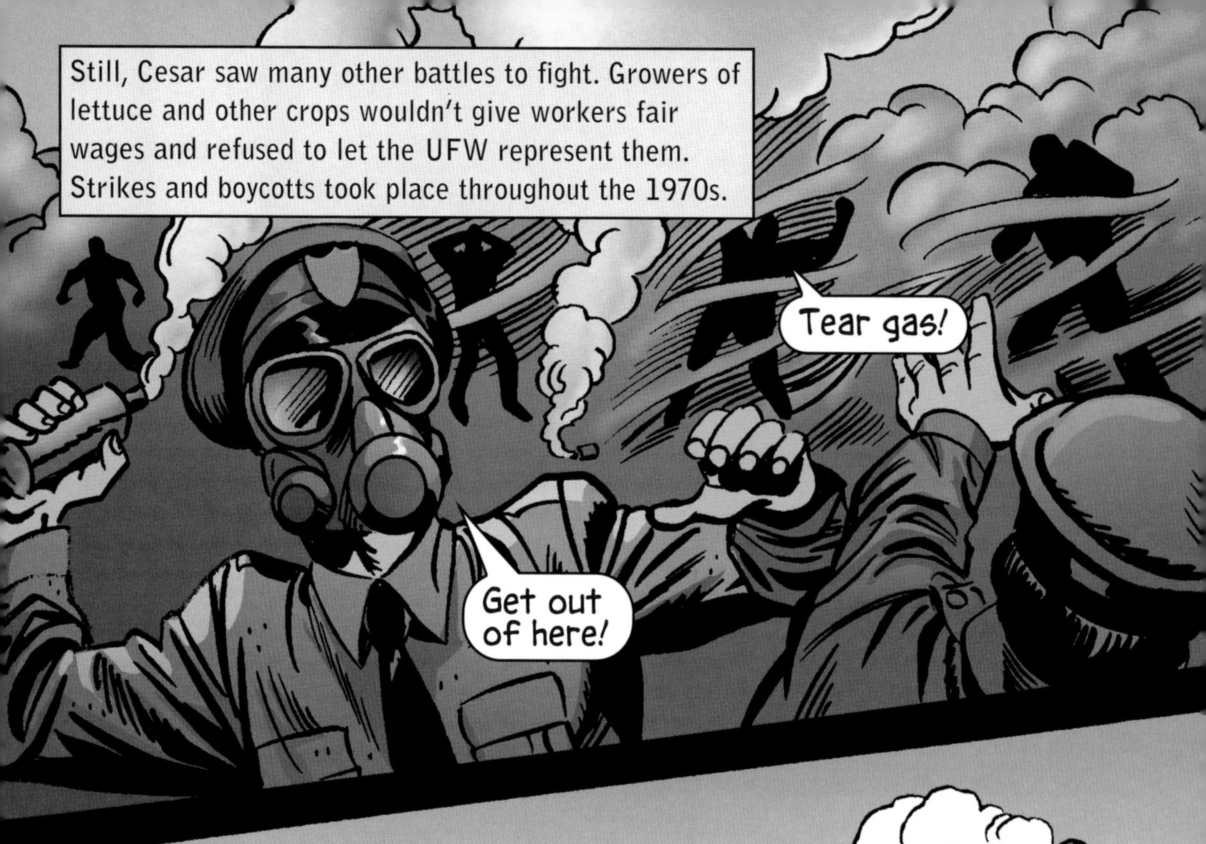
Still, Cesar saw many other battles to fight. Growers of lettuce and other crops wouldn't give workers fair wages and refused to let the UFW represent them. Strikes and boycotts took place throughout the 1970s.
Tear gas!
Get out of here!

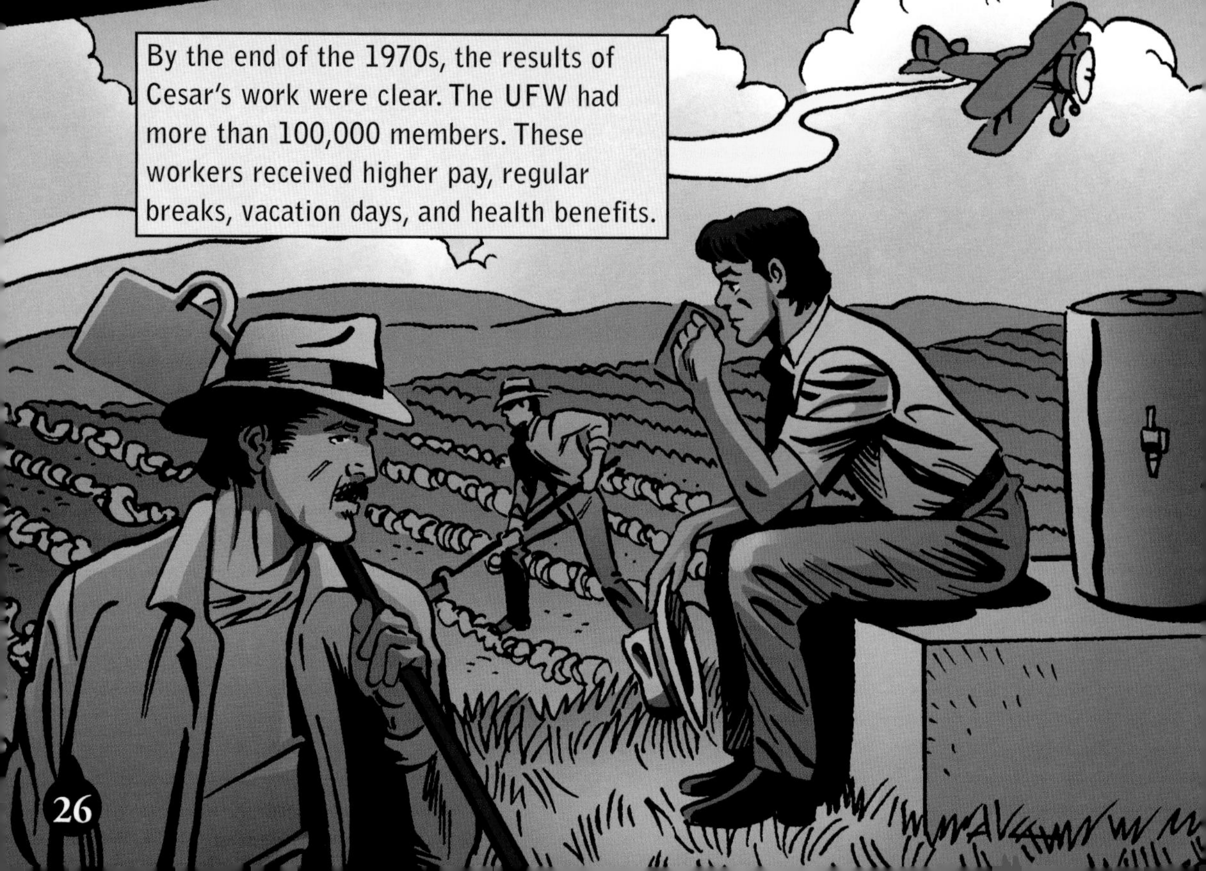
By the end of the 1970s, the results of Cesar's work were clear. The UFW had more than 100,000 members. These workers received higher pay, regular breaks, vacation days, and health benefits.

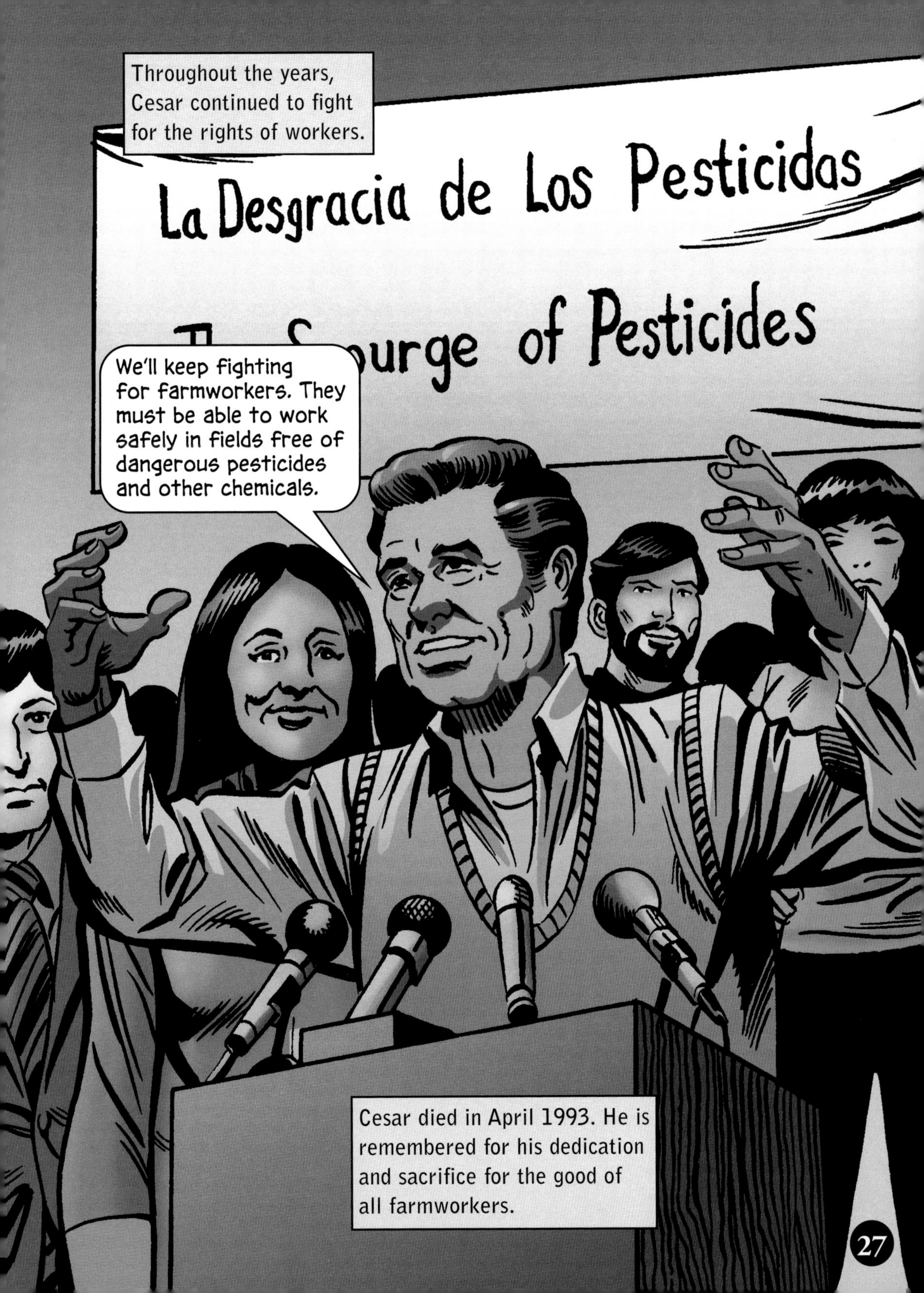
Throughout the years, Cesar continued to fight for the rights of workers.
La Desgracia de Los Pesticidas
The Scourge of Pesticides
We'll keep fighting for farmworkers. They must be able to work safely in fields free of dangerous pesticides and other chemicals.
Cesar died in April 1993. He is remembered for his dedication and sacrifice for the good of all farmworkers.

More about CESAR CHAVEZ

- Cesar Chavez was born on March 31, 1927, on a farm near Yuma, Arizona. His grandparents were Mexican immigrants.

- Cesar died in his sleep on April 23, 1993. Earlier that day, he had testified in a trial against a lettuce grower.

- Cesar served as a deckhand in the Navy from 1944 to 1946.

- Although Cesar quit school after the eighth grade, he never stopped learning. His office at UFW headquarters was filled with books on economics, philosophy, unions, and biographies on Gandhi and other world leaders. Cesar thought people should use their education to serve others.

- In 1975, Cesar helped get the Agricultural Labor Relations Act passed in California. It was the first bill of rights for farmworkers. The act protects the rights of farmworkers to unionize and select their own representatives to bargain with employers.

- In the 1980s, Cesar went on a 36-day fast to protest the use of pesticides. But few gains were made on that issue during his life.

- Cesar Chavez is remembered as a leader of all Chicanos, not just farmworkers. Many people consider Cesar Chavez to be the most important Chicano in American history.

- In 1994, President Bill Clinton awarded Cesar the Presidential Medal of Freedom, the nation's highest honor. Cesar's wife, Helen, and six of their children accepted the award for him.

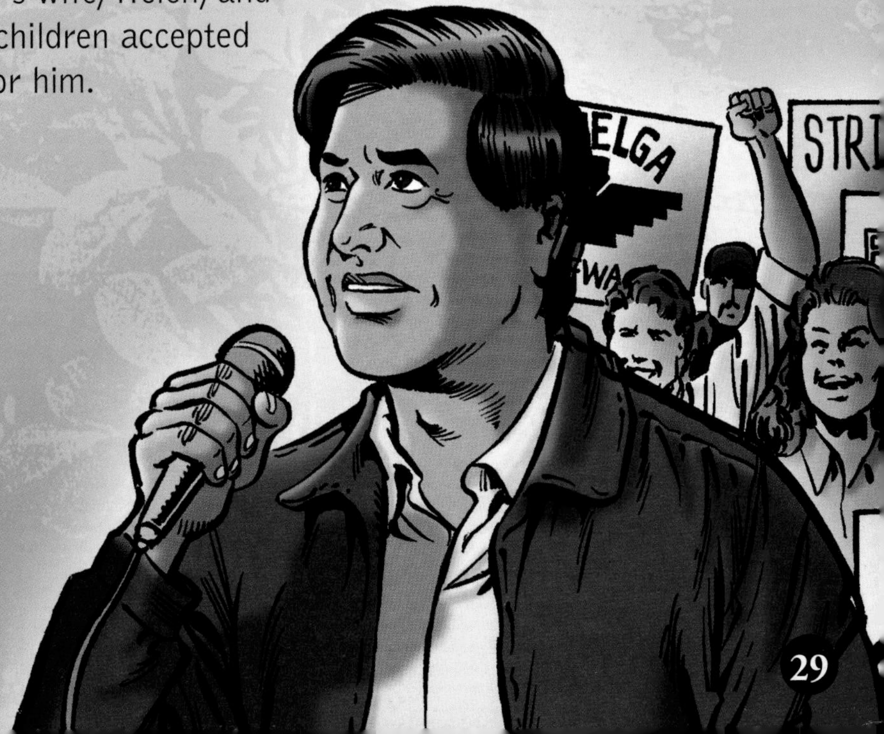
ELGA
STRI

GLOSSARY

Anglo (ANG-loh)—an American who has a European background

boycott (BOI-kot)—to refuse to buy something as a way of making a protest

Chicano (chi-KAH-noh)—an American who has a Mexican background

Filipino (fil-uh-PEE-noh)—a person from the Philippines

migrant worker (MYE-gruhnt WURK-ur)—a farm laborer who moves from place to place to harvest seasonal crops

pesticide (PESS-tuh-side)—a chemical that kills insects and other pests that eat crops

picket (PIK-it)—to protest by standing outside a place, sometimes trying to prevent people from entering

strike (STRIKE)—a refusal to work until a set of demands is met

union (YOON-yuhn)—an organized group of workers that tries to gain better pay and working conditions for workers

INTERNET SITES

FactHound offers a safe, fun way to find Internet sites related to this book. All of the sites on FactHound have been researched by our staff.

Here's how:

1. *Visit www.facthound.com*
2. Type in this special code **073684631X** for age-appropriate sites. Or enter a search word related to this book for a more general search.
3. Click on the **Fetch It** button.

FactHound will fetch the best sites for you!

READ MORE

Eddy, Susan. *Cesar Chavez*. Rookie Biography. New York: Children's Press, 2003.

Gaines, Ann. *Cesar E. Chavez: The Fight for Farm Workers' Rights*. Proud Heritage. Chanhassen, Minn.: Child's World, 2003.

Murcia, Rebecca Thatcher. *Dolores Huerta.* Latinos in American History. Bear, Del.: Mitchell Lane, 2003.

Seidman, David. *Cesar Chavez: Labor Leader.* Great Life Stories. New York: Franklin Watts, 2004.

BIBLIOGRAPHY

Clete, Daniel. "Cesar Chavez and the Unionization of California Farm Workers," in *Labor Leaders in America* by Melvyn Dubofsky and Warren Van Tine. Urbana, Ill.: University of Illinois Press, 1987.

Ferriss, Susan, and Ricardo Sandoval. *The Fight in the Fields: Cesar Chavez and the Farmworkers Movement.* New York: Harcourt Brace, 1997.

Griswold del Castillo, Richard, and Richard A. Garcia. *Cesar Chavez: A Triumph of Spirit.* Norman, Okla.: University of Oklahoma Press, 1995.

Levy, Jacques E. *Cesar Chavez: Autobiography of La Causa.* New York: W. W. Norton Company, 1975.

INDEX